I0709373

COSCOM
ENTERTAINMENT

ALSO BY A.P. FUCHS

BLOOD OF MY WORLD TRILOGY

DISCOVERY OF DEATH
MEMORIES OF DEATH
LIFE OF DEATH

UNDEAD WORLD TRILOGY

BLOOD OF THE DEAD
POSSESSION OF THE DEAD
REDEMPTION OF THE DEAD

THE AXIOM-MAN™ SAGA

(LISTED IN READING ORDER)

AXIOM-MAN
EPISODE NO. 0: FIRST NIGHT OUT
DOORWAY OF DARKNESS
EPISODE NO. 1: THE DEAD LAND
CITY OF RUIN
OF MAGIC AND MEN (COMIC BOOK)

OTHER FICTION

A STRANGER DEAD
A RED DARK NIGHT
APRIL (WRITING AS PETER FOX)
MAGIC MAN (DELUXE CHAPBOOK)
THE WAY OF THE FOG (THE ARK OF LIGHT VOL. 1)
DEVIL'S PLAYGROUND (WRITTEN WITH KEITH GOUVEIA)
ON HELL'S WINGS (WRITTEN WITH KEITH GOUVEIA)
ZOMBIE FIGHT NIGHT: BATTLES OF THE DEAD
MAGIC MAN PLUS 15 TALES OF TERROR
UNDENIABLE

ANTHOLOGIES (AS EDITOR)

DEAD SCIENCE
ELEMENTS OF THE FANTASTIC
VICIOUS VERSES AND REANIMATED RHYMES: ZANY ZOMBIE POETRY FOR THE UNDEAD HEAD
METAHUMANS VS THE UNDEAD
BIGFOOT TERROR TALES VOL. 1 (WITH ERIC S. BROWN)
BIGFOOT TERROR TALES VOL. 2 (WITH ERIC S. BROWN)
METAHUMANS VS WEREWOLVES

NON-FICTION

BOOK MARKETING FOR THE FINANCIALLY-CHALLENGED AUTHOR
CANADIAN SCRIBBLER: COLLECTED LETTERS OF AN UNDERGROUND WRITER
LOOK, UP ON THE SCREEN! - THE BIG BOOK OF SUPERHERO MOVIE REVIEWS

POETRY

THE HAND I'VE BEEN DEALT
HAUNTED MELODIES AND OTHER DARK POEMS
STILL ABOUT A GIRL

GO TO

WWW.CANISTERX.COM

&

WWW.UNDEADWORLDTRILOGY.COM

Canadian Scribbler

Collected Letters of an Underground Writer

by

A.P. FUCHS

COSCOM ENTERTAINMENT
WINNIPEG

ISBN 978-1-927339-43-5

Published by COSCOM ENTERTAINMENT
www.coscomentertainment.com

Text set in Garamond; Printed and Bound in the USA

A.P. FUCHS website: www.canisterx.com

COVER BY A.P. FUCHS
COVER PHOTOS BY A.P. FUCHS AND ROXANNE FUCHS

To scribblers everywhere, regardless how you practice your obsession.

Introduction

July 19, 2013

Dear Reader:

At thirty-two years of age, I'm not that old, but as I do get older and technology keeps changing, I'm finding I'm getting more and more old-fashioned. I have a serious love/hate relationship with the current order of the day and how we communicate with one another. It seems it's either one of two things: informal emails just bantering back and forth, or one-or-two-line text messages with shorthand writing to get our point across. I see the pros and cons of both and realize I have to keep up-to-date in certain ways so I can keep surviving in our digital era.

There was a time when people took care in how they wrote to one another. They had to. There was no instant communication in text form. Even after telephones came along, writing to one another was frequent as long distance calling was expensive. Backtrack even further, and letter writing was all you had.

That's not to say I'm not one hundred percent guilty of emailing and texting people in shorthand. I use a cell phone—like, three times a month, if that—and I do need to stay on top of emailing folks due to the nature of today's publishing climate and how my business is run. However, being a wordsmith by profession, I think we've lost something vital in how we communicate and tend to speak off the top of our heads versus actually—generally speaking—contemplating what we're saying. And if we make a mistake or our tone is misconstrued, due to the impersonal nature of email and texts, we can quickly fire off another one and correct ourselves and/or again explain what we meant right away whereas this quick fix wasn't possible before.

Onward . . .

The beauty of the publishing business is that you can make a book out of just about anything. As long as you have paper with something on it between two covers, you have a book. I didn't know letters could be collected into a book until 2005 (I think). Any time you saw someone have a collection of letters, whether in the movies or in real life, it was usually a pile of envelopes in a box kept under a mattress or on the top shelf in a dingy closet.

I learned of the collected letters format shortly after discovering *Cerebus* by Dave Sim. Once he had completed his 300-issue opus, he went about answering the mail and later collected them into a book. Two, in fact: *Collected Letters 2004*, and *Collected Letters Vol. 2*. It was while reading the former that I decided I'd hang onto correspondence worth hanging onto and one day put them all together in a book. So here we are, many years later doing just that.

For me, writing is all about honesty. I try to do that in my fiction, in my non-fiction, and even in my comics, poetry and blogging. Sort of a "This is how I feel and/or think about something and if you like it, great, and if not, I wish you well and sorry we disagree."

Letter writing is a great way for me to stay true to that ideal, and that's what is contained herein. Some are actual snail mail letters; others are emails but written like a traditional letter. The other parties' letters are not included, but my replies and/or initiations of a conversation are. I hope that by reading each you get an idea of what we were talking about and what our thoughts were on whatever subject that was brought up.

I plan on writing more letters as long as my fingers are able to type on a keyboard. If at some point I lose my hands fighting a robotic monster while saving the city as part of researching an Axiom-man story, I'll start dictating them as letter writing is something I take great joy in.

That said, I proudly present to you a series of letters spanning eight years—letter-writing gap included as there was a time my writing career in general was pretty much put on hold—covering a variety of topics as well as ones that give you a glimpse behind the curtain of a writer trying to make a living in a rapidly-changing industry.

They are printed "as written and sent" without revision or editing for this book, in keeping with the writing-as-honesty rule I try to live by.

I hope you enjoy them.

Sincerely,

A.P. Fuchs

Canadian Scribbler

Collected Letters of an Underground Writer

Darryl Sloan

Nov. 19, 2005

Dear Darryl:

Thanks again for sending me those Dvds. I'm excited to see some of the work Midnight Pictures has put out.

I also appreciate you accepting my honest review of your book, *Ulterior.* One thing I've learned in this business is the value of an honest review, especially from one's peers. I always insist to reviewers—the ones I know—that I want an honest opinion of a work otherwise I'm not interested. How else can I grow as a writer otherwise?

Anyway, to answer your question of what some of the "bad things" were, the ones that stand out in my mind as I type this are only a few. Your use of pronouns jumped out at me more than once—rather, how you named the characters throughout the narrative. Example: Eddie's dad. You kept calling him by his last name instead of, say, "Eddie's dad," or "his dad" or even by his first name, "Blake." It just read awkward and really detached me from the character of Eddie's father. I understand the need to insert a character's name throughout the text so the reader knows who's doing/saying what, and when it comes to someone's parent when their kid is in the scene, always putting "character name's dad/mom" or "his/her mom" and that's it can get kind of repetitive especially if it's a long scene. A suggestion for remedying this—and it's subjective to how it will read once the scene is typed—in the case of a parent where their kid is in the same scene, to intersperse "So-and-so's dad/mom" and "Mr./Mrs./Ms. Last name" throughout, along with some "he/she" when referring to the parent (of course, where the text warrants it). Variety works, but not too much as the reader might forget who you're talking about.

The other thing regarding pronouns is using a character's name over and over when a simple "he/she" would have been fine.

This is only a matter of taste, but like Stephen King says, sticking to a regular "he/she said" or "he/she asked" most of the time works better than "he/she queried" or "he/she exclaimed" or anything other speech tags that are not "said" or "asked."

The above are a few things that, when fixed, can really make your work come across stronger and erase any novice-like qualities that others might pick up on. Newer writers try to get fancy and put in a lot of words or variants of words because they feel it'll make the work stronger. We both know that this hardly ever works, if at all.

I hope the above is taken kindly as it was offered with a smile. I won't claim to be an expert in fiction writing (I don't think any writer can because writing, like any art form, is always in need of improvement), but I think by implementing the above, it will make a real difference once you've finished your final polished draft and you're ready to go to press.

As always, let's keep in touch.

Best,

Dave Sim

November 27, 2005

Dear Dave:

A nearly two-year belated congratulations to you and Gerhard on the completion of *Cerebus*. I'm a fairly new *Cerebus* reader, having started reading the book around the time 300 came out. So far I've read the first two phonebooks and am about a third of the way through *Collected Letters 2004* (which actually prompted my writing you today). Funnily enough, I wasn't aware that you corresponded with your readers *until* having started reading *Collected Letters 2004*. I believe I had first heard/read about *Cerebus* when I stumbled upon your self-publishing guide several years back, back when I was interested in putting out my own comic. I read it, filed it way as useful info to utilize when the time came and, as things unfolded in my own life, moved from writing and drawing comics to just writing books (although I do dabble in scripting now and then). Just recently I re-read your self-publishing guide—as I'm a self-published author myself and like to read the opinions and thoughts of like-minded individuals—and have to agree with what was presented there, namely the fact that the truth about self-publishing is finding what works best for you then utilizing that to its fullest potential. Kind of like how Bruce Lee approached his art. He took what worked, discarded what didn't, added other things that he found worked for *him* and got rid of the things that stopped working for *him*. It truly is an individual process, with the only "mandatory" things—and this goes without saying—being creating it, printing/packaging it, getting it out there. The rest and "how to" of it is finding the method(s) that work for you and running with the ball.

I also found it encouraging, of course, to read a self-publishing success story because, as said, I'm a self-publisher myself and, though not having yet achieved the same level success as you have, it's good to see what it possible if you stick to your own thing, do what works for you and go at it no holds barred. Will everyone agree? No. Like yourself, I've had my run-ins with name authors in the traditional press who, in the book biz, are of the mind that when it comes to fiction, that it's New-York-traditional-publishing-or-bust. Sign your contract, get your advance, and go home to crank out the next book. Though of course the big contract is most any struggling writer's dream, the hard reality is that getting that contract is extraordinarily difficult especially in an industry where the bottom line is all that matters and art has taken a back seat. (I'm friends with many writers who could nearly build a house out of their rejection slips.) Of course, in order for any business to function and last, the bottom line has to be kept in mind. That point is understandable otherwise any press would have gone the way of the Dodo long ago. But what drives me nuts is the fact that art has become secondary and profit is all that is cared about. That's a discussion for another time, but I do take great comfort in knowing there are small presses out there and self-published efforts by writers who put art first, new ideas first, new angles and views first, instead of writing cookie cutter fiction for the sake of the dollar and reaching more readers. Makes one wonder where the world might be at if new ideas and new thinking had been/were allowed into the popular media?

Anyway, so far, yes, I really enjoyed the first volumes of *Cerebus* and in a behind-the-scenes kind of way, it was interesting to see you grow as an artist and writer since the first issue till the end of *High Society*. I'm eager to see what happens in *Church and State* and so forth till the end. It's too bad things didn't work out with Amazon.com/.ca (I skipped forward to only that letter) as Amazon.ca is where I grab most of my reading material (namely because that's where most small presses I buy from have their catalogue listed in one convenient location). But I understand your reasoning behind your decision and, because I also run my own press, can see how their handling the back-and-forth regarding orders had caused problems. Speaking of the volumes, you had hinted in your letters collection at publishing a *Collection Essays* volume sometime in the future. Whether there still are plans for this or not, I don't know, but if there are, you can count me a customer. Since I have to get the *Cerebus* storyline in the collected volumes format, I won't be able to read the essays that filled the back part of your book for the twenty-six years it was running. I'm also a part of the Yahoo! group online and there are talks about a color volume. Whether this was your idea or the group's idea, I don't know, as I never saw the beginning of the discussion. Regardless, if it does come out, again, count me in.

Lastly—and you knew this was coming; I think you even said it yourself in one of your letters that you wait for the reader/letter writer to start commenting on your viewpoints toward the end of their letters—regarding the viewpoints (of what I've read so far) presented in *Collected Letters 2004*, I have to say that I agree with you that, in summary, society has a hard time dealing in what reality is. There is no true black and white thinking anymore. No "yes," no "no," no real right or wrong, no real true standards. That's the problem with living in a politically correct climate. Basically "everything goes" for fear of "offending" someone else. Sad but true. On an unrelated topic, I agree with your statement about a creator being judged based on the work itself and not on who they are as a creator, and being against the idea of having their work judged with the influence of who they are as a creator. It's all about the work, in the end, as that's the stuff that—God willing—will be around after you and I have left this world.

Anyway, thanks for the good reading so far. I'm sure you'll hear from me again once I'm further into the *Cerebus* storyline. All the best and I hope retirement has been treating you well.

Your fellow Canuck,

Frank Dirscherl

December 12, 2005

Dear Frank:

I suppose I owe you some gratitude, namely by your example set forth through The Wraith. What you have done with the character regarding—in short—taking a superhero creation of your own, one not crafted by any of the power players (i.e. DC or Marvel or Image or any other "known" company), trade marking it, copyrighting it, then packaging it up via various mediums and getting it out there by whatever means necessary—is nothing short of amazing. I have to admit I'm blown away by what you've accomplished so far and, I will add, you've inspired me to do the same thing with one of my own superhero creations, one I created back when I was in grade eleven long ago (so that's going back roughly eight years). The light of "Duh, I can do this, too" came on just recently, namely triggered by my current reading of Eric M. Cooper's *Knight Seeker* (I'm about 1/3 through and am really enjoying it). He's also a fellow who believes wholeheartedly in his creation and is doing his best to get his character out there by whatever means possible. From what I know, based off his web page, he's got one book, a costume and a fan film for Knight Seeker is currently underway. Prior to his book, the only exposure I've had to "independent" superheroes aside from my own were you're The Wraith and Jon Klement's Rush and the Grey Fox characters and, before both, IHero Entertainment's superhero line (it started out as a webzine but they've just gone into print) headed up by Frank Fradella (with whom I had the pleasure of working with for the Coscom Entertainment Annual No. 1: *Elements of the Fantastic*). However, you're definitely the leader in the independent superhero category given that The Wraith presently has one novel out in three editions (hardcover and paperback and eBook), one comic and one short film and a movie guide to accompany the film. Not bad and, better yet, you're got *The Wraith* #1 and 2 comics due out next year and at least one novel, *Valley of Evil*, with the possibility of other Wraith novels/stories coming out shortly after. Oh, and I forgot to mention the merchandise via cafepress.com. That's quite a bit of merchandise/product about an independent character. But again, what has impressed me is your desire and ability to get The Wraith out there without any help from any of the "powers" in the comic community. So, as mentioned above, you and the others listed have inspired me to bring my own superhero out of retirement and, if all goes well, release him into the world sometime probably late 2006.

Why I had waited so long to bring him back, I don't know. I'm keeping details under wraps for now so forgive the elusive "my hero" or "him" but I assure you he's very real and I'll be more than happy to send you some advance art (if I remember; and it's vintage art, too, as I have pics of him from back in my drawing days, so from roughly 1997-2000) prior to releasing it on his own website. I had come up with the character back in '97 and at one point wanted to write/draw/letter/publish his series on a monthly schedule via the Coscom label but, as my future unfolded, that never came to be and, for various—and upsetting—reasons, I abandoned drawing and moved into writing. I don't regret leaving my drawing behind—though I do doodle and dabble in pinups now and then—as I know my future lies in books and I believe God has something in store for me in this medium, but I often wonder what life would have been like had I stuck to drawing. Would I have got my break and found a gig(s) with DC or Marvel? Would I have managed to successfully publish a monthly comic via Coscom? My guess is no on the latter but I think I would have gotten the former if I had stuck to it.

Anyway, the point is that through my various exposures to different independent superheroes, I am reminded that anything is possible in this day and age (especially due to the advances in technology where even a small one-man operation can appear and/or produce like the big boys) and that the only thing holding anyone back from bringing their work to market is only themselves. But on the superhero front, I find it odd and surprising that I had to have others remind me that there was nothing stopping me from bringing my creation to the world. Me, above all people, someone who stands up for the independent press, for self-publishing, for creator-owned material, and who often gets in little spats with folks who believe that you have to go with the big companies otherwise your work is worth nothing.

(I can tell you stories about this but I'll save you the details; that, and I try and avoid gossip as much as possible.) What I think made it a difficult revelation is because it is superheroes we're talking about and not sci-fi or fantasy characters or mysteries or romances, etc., which is what composes virtually all of the mainstream book market save for a few exceptions (i.e. superhero movie tie-in books or a small amount of stand alone novels for Batman or Superman or the JLA, Spider-man, X-men, etc.). I suppose that since superheroes are not, on the whole, popular in mainstream publishing and since that is the field I'm in, it easily slipped my mind or didn't dawn on me that my character is worth "getting out there."

So in the end, yeah, thanks for setting a great example of how to get your own character out there and that, more importantly, there is nothing holding anyone back from doing it.

I hope you enjoy what I bring forth in 2006. Stay tuned…

Best,

Dave Sim

December 13, 2005

Dear Dave:

Thanks for taking the time to reply to my letter. Your letter is dated December 6 and I got it today, so given that it takes 3-5 business days for a letter to arrive from one Canadian address to another, it arrived right on time.

You had asked me in your letter if I use Print-on-Demand. The answer is yes. What really got me excited was that you said you might consider using it sometime in the future. I have to admit, I was tempted to give you a call and tell you everything I know about POD, but then I thought, *No, I better write it all down so that way Dave has something tangible to refer to instead.* So here we are. I will add, before I go on and on about POD, that you are more than welcome to use me as a "POD resource/info trough" as I'm quite versed in how it works, the pros and cons, and how the publishing world currently views POD. I have enclosed my business card for that purpose and printed on it is my phone number should the mood strike you. Sometimes quick questions are better answered via phone than waiting for old Postman Pat to deliver the news.

I have no idea what your POD knowledge is at present so I'll tell you the main points of what I know under the assumption that you know very little or nothing about it. That way, I figure, I'll cover all the bases.

So here we go.

Like most anything, POD has its pros and cons. Off the top of my head, unlike offset printing, your per-unit print cost doesn't change with quantity (i.e. printing one copy is going to cost you, say, $3.50 per unit, and printing one thousand copies will still cost you $3.50 per unit; I'm also speaking in US funds as that's where my current printer is located. More on that in a second). So that's a con. It is advantageous for the self-publisher who doesn't have $3500US lying around to print up a thousand copies in one go, or whatever the per-unit cost would be at a thousand. Can only afford to print a hundred or two? No problem. Get the rest when you're ready.

You're Canadian, as well as I, so this next bit might be useful. Currently I'm using a printer in the US called Lightning Source (www.lightningsource.com; feel free to have Gerhard look it up for you online; perhaps also consider giving them a call). The advantage with them is that it's true Print-on-Demand printing, meaning they follow the "print anywhere from one copy to a zillion copies" rule. In Canada, I have only found a handful of "digital printers" but each still requires a hundred-to-five-hundred-copy minimum print run. I have yet to find one that would print me up only one copy, should I ever need just one copy or even, say, ten copies. The other advantage with Lightning Source is that they're owned by Ingram, the wholesaler giant in the US, and each title you set up with them can be included in Ingram's catalogue with nothing more than the simple click of the mouse (it also lists you automatically with Baker & Taylor, one of the main library ordering systems in the States; for both the Ingram and Baker & Taylor listing, there's an annual fee; for myself, since most of my readers are in the States, utilizing US distribution works to my advantage). This helps for not only bookstore orders, but also for being listed with online retailers like Amazon.com (and listed with *any* online retailer tapped into the Ingram feed; the listing with these websites is automatic). The disadvantage when it comes to the brick and mortar stores is that though your title is "available" through Ingram, it's still up to the bookstore to order it in and unless you're an author with a name, that can be difficult unless you solicit the stores themselves via whatever marketing method(s) you choose. Another advantage to using Lightning Source is that if either an online or offline retailer orders X amount of copies of your book via Ingram, Lightning Source takes care of the fulfillment and shipping for you (which would take care of the problem you had with Amazon) and you get a check ninety days later for however many you sold (the formula being: retail price less bookstore discount (which you set) less per unit print cost equals your Net take home pay for one copy). This definitely frees up more time for the self-publisher to create future product and/or to market his/her current work and/or take care of any office work and/or fill any direct orders to both readers and libraries (that is, Canadian library orders). It is also worth noting that Canada's main wholesaler, Indigo, can also hook up to Ingram for order fulfillment (i.e. if Gerhard goes to www.indigo.ca, he can show you my own titles and the others my company has produced; this is something you'd have to set up with Indigo.ca though, the website listing; having your titles listed in the *main* Indigo system, meaning the system the major Canadian chains use to order books, is a different matter as the Indigo website is a separate system altogether; strange but true; hope that made sense). The good part about my printer being in the States is that I get paid in US dollars, which works well for me as our dollar is worth less than the American dollar. More bang for your buck, depending on how you look at it.

One of the major cons of POD is its reputation. What has happened is a bunch of vanity—or as they call themselves, "subsidy"—presses have been using POD because of its low overhead. This in turn has allowed anything under the sun to be printed, namely unedited material and terrible, terrible stories (i.e. clichéd fiction, rip-off fiction, you name it). Over the past few years bookstores have wisened up to this and are very reluctant to stock POD titles unless it's by a well-known and respectable firm like Random House (who uses primarily offset but also uses POD for its smaller titles or just to keep slow-moving titles in print, or so I've heard) or other firms like them. It's even hard for those with a small press like mine—those of us who take this business seriously and produce *edited* and quality original material—to fight our way through the mentality/stigma that POD equals, essentially, crap. In short, subsidy presses (which are bad news altogether; I used one for my first book and, man, what a HUGE mistake; it was a nightmare start to finish) have given POD a bad name. Same with other outfits like lulu.com where, though there is no cost to you to set up your title, *anything* can be printed and there is no monitoring of content. Lulu.com makes their money by charging very high per unit costs to their authors (i.e. what would normally be a $4 POD book, they would charge around $9, roughly). Yikes! I think their service is a great one in allowing an author to "test the waters" with his/her work, but I really do wish there was some sort of standard one had to adhere to regarding what is published (I'm mainly referring to having it mandatory your material is edited). What needs to happen, in my opinion, is for these companies to be exposed for what they are and, further, shut down. I could tell you countless stories about dozens of authors whose dreams have been crushed by these so called "publishers." ("Publishers" who, even after charging an author an arm and a leg to "publish" their book, only pay out to their authors a small royalty of 10-20% Net.) I think a writer (or comic book creator) has only two options when it comes to seeing their work in print. Either a) go the traditional route via a small or large press or, b) self-publish the work via your own company. The option of subsidy/vanity publishing shouldn't be there. Too many people get hurt (I was one of them). The only "out of house," in my opinion, that a self-publisher should do is pay the printing bill. And even then, if you had a million or two to spare, then by all means get your own printing press. (Provided you'll recoup the cost, of course.)

One of the downsides to POD is the per unit print cost, which, as mentioned, is a flat cost per book regardless of quantity printed. I look at the justification (perhaps just for my own comfort) of the higher per unit cost like this: a) Lightning Source is fulfilling all my wholesale orders for me so they should be compensated for that (fair is fair), b) though there are no physical books until the book is actually "printed when ordered," they are acting like a virtual warehouse so instead of spending X amount per book housing them somewhere (like the big publishers do; or they buy their own huge warehouses or pay for "land" in another warehouse), I give the printer a little bit for that as well. So, if you took away those two costs, I suppose my per unit print cost would be about what it would cost via offset printing, again depending on quantity produced.

In the end, yeah, if you're looking to sell five hundred to around a thousand copies of something, POD is definitely a good choice and, as said, with Lightning Source, most of your fulfillment is taken care of (that is except for direct market orders and any Canadian library orders you might get). Otherwise I'd stick with offset.

I hope the above information was helpful, Dave, and like I said, my door is open to any questions you might have.

I hope this letter finds you well. Say hello to Gerhard for me. Thanks again. Keep in touch.

Sincerely,

PS. I just finished watching the *Ye Bookes of Cerebus* Dvd the other night. Jeff Tundis sent me a copy. Very informative, and the Cerebus artwork—from what I could see on the Dvd—was truly amazing. The exhibit runs till end of January. How is it going so far?

Matt Schwartz
Shocklines.com

December 18, 2005

Dear Matt:

I'm not really sure where to begin other than to say thank you for your loyalty as a customer this past year. I sincerely appreciate you taking a shot with an unknown press and especially with authors who don't carry the same name power as your top sellers do. I remember the Red Light District interview/chat you did and really liked what you had to say about the small press, most notably the part about supporting and touting lesser-known books by lesser-known authors. You're truly a champion in that regard and I want to say thanks for that.

I've always been a believer that small press and self-published work are the hidden gems in the publishing industry and it's really good to know (and use) a bookstore like Shocklines.com to find these items as they're pretty much impossible to find in the major chains. The "hidden gem" theory also holds true in that many small press published folks have then found their way into the big NY firms and, in turn, brought a spotlight on smaller releases. It's good for everybody and this year the all-for-one atmosphere has really shone through. I'm not sure if you've picked up on it but I certainly have. And I think my "believer" status regarding the small press has now turned to "big believer." Small press stuff, for the most part, is far better than most of what the larger firms are putting out. I'm not saying every book coming out of NY is cookie-cutter fiction, but you have to admit a large portion of it is. Makes one wonder what the publishing biz would be like if every Joe and Jane Public knew about the small press and that they could find unique stories there instead of reading the same author tell the same story dozens of times. But I'm not going to complain.

In '06 there'll be some changes to Coscom Entertainment, namely the decrease in books released and the shifting of gears toward my getting back to work on my own career. I have a couple releases for myself planned—self-published efforts for works that require a large degree of creator control; there will also be my first lettered edition of an upcoming work—and also some neat things happening on the traditional front.

It's a strange business but I'm glad there's a bookstore like Shocklines.com that breaks open the avenues to works that are worth reading and works that, in my opinion, are often stronger than the more traditional pop-fiction we're seeing nowadays. My view can also be slightly jaded as I live in Canada and our bookstore climate is different than the USA. We very much rely on what's "in the stores" and that's about it. Thank God for the Internet.

Have you ever tried writing anything yourself? I mean, something that you could really go for it with? I know Shocklines.com has its own press so even if you didn't want to traditionally publish it, you could always put it out yourself. You're popular enough to guarantee more than just a handful of sales. I'm betting 300-500 copies would be a conservative estimate. I strongly encourage you to try and put something out there as I'd love to read one of your stories.

As I write this you have a standing order for my *The Way of the Fog*. I'll be signing and shipping them Monday so you should receive them within 5-10 business days from then.

Thanks again, Matt, and Merry Christmas!

Sincerely,

George Clayton Johnson

December 19, 2005

Dear George Clayton Johnson:

It was good speaking with you last week and congratulations again on the re-optioning of *Logan's Run*. I'm also excited that Bryan Singer is involved because I love his previous work—though there are a couple films of his I have yet to see—and am looking forward to his *Superman Returns* in June 2006. (I'm a huge Superman fan.)

As a small disclaimer, this letter is written from one writer to another instead of from publisher to writer.

Please find enclosed a copy of my epic fantasy entitled, *The Way of the Fog*, which is the first volume in a planned 6-8 books series called, *The Ark of Light*.

A brief history of the novel (and my publishing history):

The Way of the Fog bounced around in my head for a few years before being committed to paper, lingering in the back of my mind as I produced my second and third novels. It was originally planned to be published as a limited edition hardcover, a kind of "gift" to my readers who have been following my other works. *The Ark of Light* series serves as a backbone to all my other work and answers the big question of why things happen as they do in my books, answered independently of the resolutions and answers put forth in whatever work of mine a reader is reading. After positive feedback from readers and reconsideration of my own, I realized that my story had mass market potential so as it stands right now, I'm in the process of selling the mass market rights to the book. There is something "up in the air" regarding my goal to see it produced on a mass market scale but it's so early in the process that anything can happen. I have backup plans should it not pan out. I am, of course, hoping it does. The second volume to the series is roughly a third complete at around 80,000 words. I plan on finishing volume two in 2006 and, depending on how things go on the mass market front, again release a limited edition of the book—that is, book two—sometime in 2007.

Though I'm a huge advocate for self-publishing and the independent press, I'm also aware that there are limits to the exposure and amount of readers those avenues can provide. If I am to one day realize my goal of writing novels for a living, I need to break in to the mass market circles. I don't know how well versed you are in today's publishing climate for an unknown writer, but it truly is difficult for an unknown to get his/her foot in the door and perhaps even more so nowadays than, say, twenty-some-odd years ago when Stephen King got his big break. (He is also one of two people who inspired me to start writing in the first place; him and Alan Moore, the comic book writer.) Sure, there are unknowns picked up regularly by New York, but when you compare that number to the number of writers trying to get a shot, the ones picked up are pretty much just a handful in comparison. However, I believe in hard work and persistence and God's blessing, so I'm hoping that those three combined will result in a mass market deal for *The Way of the Fog*, in turn opening the door to reaching more readers than I could manage on my own. Should a mass market deal also arise, I'm hoping that by my success it'll bring a spotlight on self-published works and small press novels as there are truly so many good stories being produced in those circles that Joe Reader will never discover simply because a small press author doesn't have the same distribution and marketing access/ability the big New York firms can provide. It's a matter of dollars and cents when it comes right down to it.

The reason I had begun self-publishing my own work, as I had mentioned in one of our telephone conversations, was because of that little thing called a rejection slip. But what I gained in return was an interest in how books are produced from novel idea (no pun) to actual printed book and the potential a self-published work can have if done correctly and how such a publishing method can at least serve as a starting point in any novelist's career. Self-publishing also inspired me to aid others who were having a hard time landing a mass market publisher not necessarily because their story was terrible, but because it wasn't "marketable" on the scale mass market publishers require to make back their investment and then profit. When you had commended me on my efforts in what I'm trying to accomplish with Coscom Entertainment, your words meant a lot as it felt really good for someone to recognize what I was attempting to do. I believe all books deserve a chance in that if they were important enough to "lock down" on paper, they are important enough to be read even if that readership is as small as, say, a group of family and friends. But I'm also aware—and know—that some novel attempts need work before they're publish-ready, but I always encourage those writers to keep trying and suggest to them where they can make improvements so that they may take those suggestions as they will when working on their next manuscript. Again, in a publishing climate where you have to either be an already-selling name to land a book deal or to have-been-published-to-be-published (the famous publishing Catch 22), I'm doing my best to offer a means to authors with publishable material to get their work out there without them having to resort to a vanity or subsidy publisher.

Anyway, I didn't mean to talk about myself but I also wanted to share where I'm coming from and what my goals are with *The Way of the Fog* and my company. I truly hope you enjoy the tale and I look forward to your comments should you have any.

Happy Holidays and warmest regards,

Eric M. Cooper

December 22, 2005

Dear Eric:

I had finished reading your novel, *Knight Seeker,* a couple of days ago. Overall I really enjoyed it. He reminds me of a suped-up Spider-man and I thought that blending superhero and science fiction together gave it a freshness I haven't seen in a while.

It's only been recently that I've indulged in the world of the independent superhero, but from what I can see based on your book and your website, you're headed down the right track in helping bring your character to the masses.

I do have a few comments that might strengthen your next outing so if you're open to feedback, please let me know.

Take care and all the best in 2006.

Sincerely,

Frank Dirscherl

December 24, 2005

Dear Frank:

It's the morning of Christmas Eve and instead of sleeping, I'm writing back to your reply to my email dated December 12.

I found it interesting when you said an editor contacted you and wanted to work with you on The Wraith. How did he hear about you, or do you think he was trying to "cash in" on what's no doubt going to be a big thing? I also found it even more interesting that he wanted more money to work "with you" on the character and then wanted to change The Wraith into something different/something he wasn't. It's a strange business. An editor's job is to take a writer's work and clear out any grammar issues, punctuation issues, discontinuities, character contradictions, telling versus showing, etc., and basically fine-tune what you have already written. I don't agree with an editor revamping a work to make it more marketable because by doing that, you're robbing the work itself, from *being* itself. Whether that was this fellow's intention or not is anyone's guess.

Have you looked into any other independent superhero comics or novels? Any others worth getting into?

Merry Christmas! Hope it's a good one.

Sincerely,

Ps. I'm looking forward to the Dvd of *The Wraith: Eyes of Judgment*, provided it's on time. I'm also thrilled that I'm a part of the documentary on its Special Features.

D.F. Lewis

December 30, 2005

Dear D.F.:

Thanks for starting the "What Does 'Published' Actually Mean" conversation. I didn't realize it would get into the expanded discussion that it currently is, but I'm glad it turned out that way. I always find it interesting when such threads start, as it really forces you to look at your own career and how you are currently going about doing things—truly find out if what you're doing is "right" or "wrong" or "somewhere in between." Such discussions also serve as a kind of checkpoint in you're own thinking and forces you to reassess what you believe and/or know to be true.

I'm not surprised it almost got into a heated debate but self-publishing discussions tend to do that. In the end—and like I always say—you got to find what works for you in this business and go with it and tweak it along the way. I'm also not opposed to being proved wrong about my ideas about publishing, the publishing business itself or if my stance on certain issues is unwarranted or half wrong/half right.

I think the fact you published *The Hawler* on your blog was a very daring move…and also an inspiring one.

Sincerely,

D.F. Lewis

December 31, 2005

Dear D.F.:

Thanks for the quick reply.

I did get a little tongue-tied/confusing, didn't I? The thing is, when it comes to any publishing discussion, namely one dealing with self-publishing or arguing "which is the better way," such a topic always ends up going in a million different directions. What would be great is if there was a way to talk about only ONE aspect of a specific publishing method, go over the pros and cons, then start a new topic dealing with the next ONE and so forth. I think more valuable info would be shared/come forth as a result.

Perhaps in the future.

Sincerely,

Darryl Sloan

January 4, 2006

Dear Darryl:

Again, glad you liked *A Red Dark Night* overall despite some of its lesser points. It was one of those books that, as per its intro, was written as a tribute to cheesy B-horror and was meant to be one of those simple, fun stories. It also was my first solo effort self-publishing hence a few of its layout issues, the mismatching quotation marks and such. I plan on revising/re-editing it when I publish its sequel, *A Red Dark Day,* either later this year or early 2007 because, as you know, the ending is very open ended/sequel-ready. On the plus side, it helped me learn how to properly put out a book on my own (see *April, Magic Man, The Way of the Fog,* etc.). Funnily enough, *A Red Dark Night* remains my bestseller so far. I think most people dig it because the story is—as I've been told—very cinematic (whatever that means because all stories are "cinematic" to some degree; they all contain scenes that play in your head like a movie). For the revamp, I'll be removing the sex stuff because I've decided to use my writing for God and, of course, the sex stuff isn't very honoring to Him. Likewise I'll see what I can do about any language that might be in there (I can't remember if I put in swears or not as it's been about a year and a half since I read the book).

Thanks for the recommendation for *The Elements of Style.* It's on my bookshelf, actually. Very helpful indeed.

You don't like my "pen name"? Originally I was going to use my first and last name, but then way back when *A Stranger Dead* came out it was a last minute decision to switch it. I think R.A. Salvatore was the reason I went the "initial" route. All I remember was I thought the initial-only thing was cool. I've thought about switching it to my full name now and then, but A.P. Fuchs is what I'm known by and if I switch it, I'd have to start from the ground up marketing/branding-wise. Partially, anyway.

I tried running those Dvds you sent me on my player at home but my player (about 7 years old) doesn't recognize the format. I'll try them again the next time I'm at my folks. Theirs might be able to play them.

Thanks again. How's your new novel coming?

Best,

Eric M. Cooper

January 6, 2006

Dear Eric:

I apologize for the late reply. Had a busy Christmas Season this past year. Anyway, as per your reply, I wouldn't presume to ask you to make any "changes" to your current or future novels, but rather I have a few suggestions that will help strengthen your book(s) as a whole.

I'm assuming *Knight Seeker* was your first novel, or at least the first one written with a serious eye for writing and/or making a potential career out of it. A few of the things I found in your book which are telltale signs of a first novel are things that most first time novelists do, so no worries. (I made the same mistakes on my first *two* novels; fortunately, only one of them saw print though it will be pulled from print shortly for reworking. The other is currently on hold until I find the time to revise it.)

Anyway, quite simply, the use of multiple points-of-view in any given scene is one of them. Very seldom does a multi-point-of-view novel work, meaning one where every scene is told from everybody's perspective. I have yet to read a novel that has pulled this off successfully. May I suggest that the next time you write a scene, that it is told from only *one* person's point-of-view/perspective. After all, that is how we live our lives. You live your life from your side of the fence and I live mine from my side. You only know things about me from what I tell you and vice versa. You may switch points-of-view with each scene, but not during the *same* scene unless it is broken up by, typically, three stars (i.e. ***). But be careful where you place the asterisks so that you don't break up a scene too badly just to switch from one person's view to the next and then back again. See any book on your shelf for what I mean.

Another thing was using pronouns too often when a simple he/she, him/her or his/hers would do just fine. Repeating someone's name over and over again in a chunk of narrative begins to hurt the reader's "ears" after awhile.

The above is all said warmly and with encouragement. But I really think that if even the above two were applied to future installments of *Knight Seeker*, I believe the story will come out on "the next level" and really add a sense of weight to what you're trying to accomplish with your character.

You had asked me what my lifestyle is currently like. I'm not quite I sure I understand what you mean so I'll leave that alone for now.

If you have any questions on the above or wish to correspond more, by all means, my door's wide open.

Sincerely,

Douglas Clegg

January 18, 2006

Dear Doug:

A few days back I finished reading *The Hour Before Dark*. Well done. Truly.

A few highlights (referring to the Leisure paperback edition):

On page 31, Nemo's real name: Fergus. Honestly, I've never heard of that name until I read your book. Very cool of you on choosing an usual name other than, say, Chris or Mike or Joe.

On page 67, I really enjoyed—of all things—the description of Nemo's mother's hair. Beautiful.

On page 69, the statement about real love sometimes meaning letting love fly. Truer words have never been spoken. On a personal note, this statement touched me in a special way as it's something I've struggled with for a long time regarding someone.

The whole of chapter fifteen: so much of myself in this chapter (save for the ending where the scene switches away from Nemo and Pola). It reminded me of some of the main points I was driving at in my novel, *April*, written under my pseudonym, Peter Fox. My whole novel drew from my feelings toward someone from long ago and in chapter fifteen in your book, as Nemo and Pola found themselves in each other again, well, my heart stung with fond memories and all the fuzzies that go with it.

Page 192, Nemo's ritual of writing out whatever was in his head before getting down to business. Is this a practice of yours?

On page 360, the comment about the less said about a writing project, the more urgent it seems. I couldn't agree more and I try, for my own stories, to stick to Stephen King's rule of "writing with the door closed" for my first draft. It's just between me and the computer, no one else, and by keeping it "secret," the story always calls to me to come and finish writing it.

I'll admit that I owe you an apology regarding the book's ending. Before you find out who really killed Nemo's father, I honestly thought it was going to be his mother's ghost. My first thought was, *How predictable*. But when the true killer was revealed, wow, a sigh of relief. Thanks for throwing me for a spin.

Thanks for the great chapter endings/the endings of the mini-chapters inside the chapters. Cliffhanger endings are a must in fiction and yours did the trick of forcing me into reading the next one. The sense of history and real-life-weight of the Raglan family was a nice touch. To me, that's what gave them that final push from names on a page to real-deal characters.

There was also a touch of Stephen King in the writing, the two things I noticed being—and I know he's not the only one who does this—the use of brackets in the narrative for "on the side" comments. It's in King's work that I've noticed it the most. The other King touch I noticed was the way you made a few characters—ones that are not of the main cast nor even secondary characters—back up-back up characters?—when you mentioned them off the cuff, you still added a sense of depth to them, however briefly, really rounding things out.

Thanks for a great tale.

Sincerely,

K.J. Anderson

January 20, 2006

Dear K.J.:

Thank you for forwarding me a copy of your novelization of *The League of Extraordinary Gentlemen* movie. I look forward to reading it. I'm a huge fan of the comic book series (well, at least the first graphic novel; I have yet to buy the others). It'll be interesting to see how close your novelization is to the movie as, to be perfectly honest, I've never read a movie adaptation before so don't know if such a book is word-for-word, scene-for-scene as the film, or if the author also ends up adding some stuff to the story that either wound up on the cutting room floor or is a product of his/her imagination.

Thank you again. Feel free to keep in touch.

Sincerely,

Dave Sim

January 23, 2006

Dear Dave:

I apologize for my delay in answering your letter dated Dec. 31, 2005. January has been a very busy month for me both personally and professionally. I'm also susceptible to migraines and have had a couple this month. If you've ever had one, you know they can cripple you if not caught in time.

To clarify my previous point on a flat-rate-per-unit when it comes to a POD book, that flat rate varies from project to project based on that book's page-length (i.e. some POD books are the previously mentioned $3-something per copy, others are $4-something, etc., all based on final page count). I won't pretend to know the ins and outs of printing and printing technologies, but I assume POD books, once setup with a POD printer, are sold to the publisher at a flat rate per unit because the publisher can order any number of quantities at any one time, 1 or 1000 or even a weird number like 431. In offset, as you know, the more paper used and the more ink used, the cheaper it is per "part" as a whole hence the ability to lower the final per unit cost of the printed product (usually ordered in blocks of 500, if I understand offset correctly). I wouldn't necessarily say POD's flat-rate-per-unit is a "computer thing" though, unless I misinterpreted your meaning. Or if "computer thing" was meant as a reference to

POD technology, which is basically computer-based because all it really is, is a computer hooked up to a giant photocopier, then I understood your meaning. Ah, the joys of letter of correspondence.

Likewise I feel I should clarify the statement that POD books are usually not edited. This is the result of—as mentioned in my previous letter—subsidy/vanity POD outfits accepting any material under the sun regardless of literary quality. If the manuscript is riddled with errors, who cares so long as you have the money to pay them to set it up in their system for you. Sad but true. It could be the greatest story in the universe, but if every sentence starts with a lowercase letter, hey, you got the money? Great! We'll print it.

Interpretation writing. Ha ha! More like nowadays it's "interpretation living" for the most part given our politically correct society based on, as you mentioned, "You know what I mean." The absence of clarity in our country (and throughout the world) astounds me daily and I feel a swell of pity for us as a race because (as mentioned in my first letter to you), our concept of black and white, right and wrong, yes and no—has gone the way of the dodo. It will also lead to our eventual undoing because if history is any indicator, any time a society has let itself go soft on what is and what isn't correct/right/proper/fill-in-the-blank, it eats itself from within and falls. If you've noticed, more people today are pressing the "to each his/her own" attitude than ever before. I wonder what spawned this or, better, why it's suddenly more vocal today than at any other time in history? Any thoughts?

Have you given further consideration to a *Collected Essays* volume? I'd very much be interested should it occur.

Anyway, I'm off to go finish up preparing dinner so I'll leave you for now.

Take care.

I might be phoning in an order for the next *Cerebus* volume on my list, but I might also get my copy via another means (being the on-line shopper that I am). Just a heads up.

Sincerely,

Patrick Winceton

February 3, 2006

Dear Patrick:

Thanks for dropping me a line. It's cool to hear you have an interest in self-publishing. Right off the hop I'll tell you it isn't an easy road and it can be an expensive one (so be sure to weigh your project carefully), but it can be well worth it and rewarding if done properly.

The printer I'm using at present is Lightning Source (www.lightningsource.com) which is a print-on-demand printer. The reason I chose them aside from the quality product they produce was the fact that they're owned by Ingram, which in turn allows for easy listing at online retailers like Amazon.com and makes the books easily orderable via brick and mortar stores in the USA. They also handle the fulfillment of these orders. For hardbacks, they do dust jacket and casebound books. If you're looking at something fancier, like a leatherbound volume, I would suggest consulting printing companies in your area, see if they do that kind of work and start getting quotes from them.

For a magazine of the size you're talking about, with Lightning Source it would cost about $2.50-$2.60 a copy. Then you'd just times that out over however many you need to print. There's also setup fees for each title you do and these fees vary from project to project but they're very affordable.

For small presses, the easiest and cheapest way to promote is online. I had written a book called *Book Marketing for the Financially-challenged Author*, which basically shows you how to market your book (or magazine) effectively for about the cost of a meal. I have some copies on hand if you're interested.

My door's open should you have any further questions. Thanks again for contacting me.

Best,

Brian Keene

February 5, 2006

Dear Brian:

Just read your post on your new blog, World Domination 101. It was a very well put together piece and your homework assignment of thinking about why you want to be a writer and why you want to make a living writing fiction—I had to comment on it. This, by far, is a key issue that *must* be addressed by every writer no matter where they are on the publishing chain. It is also the same question/issue I put forth to any writer who emails me/asks me for advice on publishing (i.e. my thoughts on getting published traditionally or self-publishing). The more time I spend in the publishing world and the more I learn about the process, the more I am convinced that this business is about finding what works for you and running with it. Which brings us back to that central issue about why you write and why you want to make a living doing it. If you answer that, you've already taken a huge step toward accomplishing that goal, whatever it may be.

Writing for fun aside—that is just writing because you have to but leaving your finished and edited stories in the drawer—knowing where you want to wind up on the publishing scene involves finding out how the system works and the how you can make that system work for you.

Some of my thoughts being:

If you're looking to become the next John Grisham or Stephen King, then for sure, query those agents, query New York, keep throwing your line out to the big fish until one of them bites. It's the only way to hit it on a mass market scale and make a decent-to-good living doing this. It also paves the way, as you know, for subsidiary sales.

If you're content with/happy to stay in/wanting only to achieve success in the small press, then you can find yourself a traditional small press publisher or, perhaps—and *only* if you know what you're doing—put the work out yourself. (As I've often touted, my personal experience has been, both exposure and monetary return-wise, of traditional small press publishing and self-publishing being interchangeable terms.) Of course this little statement opens up a potentially interesting and friendly discussion (which I'm open to having with you if you're so inclined) of the pitfalls of self-publishing. I do agree that it's definitely not for everyone and, more often than not, is the path to doom for most. It's an uphill battle the whole way. However, history has dictated that successes have come from the self-publishing pool albeit few and far between. If any writer asks me if they should self-publish, I always refer them back to that first question of "why are you doing this/what do you hope to achieve and why?" I then lay out the hard facts of self-publishing and that if they choose to go that route, they better be sure they've done their homework and are well aware they are signing off on a death sentence if they pursue that course. But I still stand by that self-publishing—whatever your reason for doing it—can be a good way to get your stuff out there and—without the aid of subsidy or vanity presses—can be used as a small press stepping stone on to bigger and better things. If the writer isn't prepared for hard work, industry prejudice and all the rest, then I tell them going traditional will be much easier on them—should they get the contract—and they can spend all their time writing instead of doing the other tasks involved in book production and marketing.

Anyway, without going off on a long ramble, I put forth a cyber handshake to your World Domination entry because without that first key question being answered and fully understood by any writer—they won't get far, if anywhere at all.

I hope to hear back from you. You'll definitely being hearing from me as I want to talk about *The Rise and Fall of Babylon.*

Sincerely,

Ps. I just got an email today that my copy of *The Rising* is on re-order from Indigo.ca. Looking forward to it.

Darryl Sloan

February 6, 2006

Dear Darryl:

Glad you loved the most recent *Coscomment* article, "Outside the Ring." I may have taken a chance with posting it, but also to stay true to the spirit of the article, it was something that had to be said. I'm all for sincere congratulatory remarks on messageboards, pats on the back and all the rest, but I am opposed to using what are supposed to be honest statements as stepping stones just to serve yourself. Though I didn't mention it in the article, I'm frustrated, too, with authors who only post when they got a product to sell or only have something to say about themselves. That's borderline spam in my opinion. Writing communities are meant to be what their name implies: a community of writers getting together to talk about their craft, the ups and downs, what they're currently reading and working on, and just general chitchat. I appreciate the fact that if you have your sights set on the big contract that networking with established professionals will help you get there. By all means. That's just how the system works both in the publishing biz and in whatever industry you happen to be working in. It is my feeling that despite the publishing business being very much a highly competitive, dog-eat-dog one, it those who approach it with sincerity, humbleness and perseverance who will eventually get to where they want to be. There's something about the authentic individual that sticks with us, that makes them stand out above the rest and I sense that it is those who will rise to the top. All in due time, of course.

Messageboards and online groups can serve as a marketplace, but it shouldn't be treated solely like one. It is those who do so that, from what I've seen thus far, seem to be stuck in that rut of catering only to writers in turn making those writers their only audience. As mentioned in the article, those writers represent only a small, small percentage of the actual reading public out there. Go after the reader, man, and the rest will follow suit.

If you know anyone who you feel might benefit from *Coscomment*, feel free to pass the URL on. Thanks in advance.

On a side note, I caught your post on your blog about oneyearbibleonline.com. Thanks. I've finding the system of a bit from the Old Testament, a bit from the New, and a Psalm and Proverb a day really effective. I had an interesting answered prayer experience today. Some might call it mere coincidence but I'm reluctant to think so. I had to step out to pick up some infant formula for my son. As I was driving to the store, I prayed that I would bump into someone I know there (simply because I love bumping into people I know while out and about). Sure enough, I ran into my father there. As it so happened, the store was sold out of the formula brand my wife and I buy so I went to the other Superstore not too far away, found the formula and as I was making my way to the cashier, I ran into a guy and his wife whom I had gone to church with (back when I went to my parents' church). What a blessing! I found it especially comforting because at present I believe I'm going through a spiritual testing period where God is choosing to remain silent on some things. I know full well He does so for a reason and I sense it's just the season I'm in right now. But to have Him answer that prayer today was an exciting reminder that's He's always there from me even though sometimes—and though this is the enemy putting it in my head—I think that He's forgotten about me or what I need help in.

Anyway, I heard back from Bantam last week regarding the mass market rights to my novel, *The Way of the Fog.* I received a personal reply from the editor there as opposed to the standard form rejection that you usually receive 9.9 times out of 10 from mass market firms. That in and of itself was encouraging. Unfortunately he/she had to pass but solely on the basis that though he/she found the premise very interesting, it wouldn't be a good fit for Bantam's fantasy line (Spectra). Fair enough. There is a religious element to it and my hope is that someday it will get picked up by a mass market firm because I want to use it as an avenue to tell others about Jesus. I am currently awaiting reply from three top New York-based agents so if it's His will that I should sign with one of them, great. If not, I'm confident that if He wants it to be published, He'll pave the way and I have nothing to worry about save for doing my part of making New York aware of the book's existence to the best of my ability. As a prayer request, can you ask Jesus that His will be done for my series?

Your brother in Christ,

Ps. What does the timeline for your new novel look like? I need a Sloan fix.

Erin Lyss

February 13, 2006

Dear Erin:

Sorry for the late reply. I'm really glad you love *The Way of the Fog.* I'm really proud of it both in its scope and story, but also in that it represents how much I've grown as a writer since *A Stranger Dead* (did you catch the *A Stranger Dead* reference in the beginning of *The Way of the Fog*?).

What I'm truly hoping for with *The Ark of Light* series is an opportunity to share the Gospel with a wide audience. I'm in the process of trying to sell the mass market rights to it now, in fact. I'm trusting that if God wants the novel out there on a wider scale that He'll make it happen. I just got to do my part in making those "higher up" in the industry aware of the novel's existence.

When you finish the book, you should be able to see where I'm going with it in regards to introducing to the characters and their world the truth about the Black and the White and who/what those forces represent and the reality of those forces. What I want to drive home as a major point in later volumes in the *seriousness* of one's salvation and how one can obtain salvation through Christ. We live in a world where the idea of God and Jesus and the devil is kind of washed over and isn't taken as seriously as it should. A lot of people, in fact, just chalk up the Bible to a piece of legend and/or myth and not an actual piece of history like it is. The Bible, after all, is a history book and not just some "Christian fairytale."

Anyway, if you don't mind, please add the above to your prayers and that His Will be done for the series. That's all I'm after in regards to reaching a wider audience.

Love to hear your thoughts once you've finished the book.

Sincerely,

Dave Sim

February 17, 2006

Dear Dave:

There are services offered from POD subsidy outfits for the editing of the books, but this is at the author's option. Due to the extremely high prices for this service (typically the subsidy outfit has a pool of freelance editors they utilize for it—no doubt the subsidy outfit overcharges so they, too, make a profit on top of whatever the editor is making) most authors neglect this service. Some simply don't understand the necessity for editing and others, as mentioned, just can't afford it. A smart author recognizes that no matter how good of a job they've done on their book that that book still needs to have a set of eyes that are not theirs to go over it. Editors come in two varieties: the copyeditor (who checks everything from simple punctuation and spelling to the stuff of content—continuity, clichéd sentences, inconsistent character behavior—the deeper stuff) and the proofreader (who only checks for spelling and basic grammatical issues and leaves the deeper stuff alone). Most editors charge either by the word or by the page. For myself, I charge by the word as that method is more accurate in terms of the actual work needed to be done on a particular piece as precise word count does vary from page to page. I think most authors would go for an editor, one they'd have to hire, based on a) the editor's experience/reputation, b) the price for the service of either copyediting or proofreading. And if one is putting out their own work, affordability is a huge factor. I would ill-advise an author to utilize an editor suggested by a subsidy outfit (if I could not convince them to steer clear of the subsidy/vanity outfit altogether) as I've heard horror stories how even the editors these places use are of the sub par variety.

As a point of interest, I maintain a weekly webblog (blog) at http://coscomentertainment.blogspot.com The first chunk of entries deal with self-publishing, the bigger issues. (After all, you can fill a whole book on the topic of self-publishing.) One of them discusses the importance of editing. Consider having Gerhard visit the site for you and print off the articles for your own reading. Perhaps we can get a dialogue going on those items.

Your reply to my question regarding where all this "gray stuff" may have come from is very true. The Civil Rights movement having been indirectly responsible is a good assessment. The summation of your point is applicable to how we as a people (on the whole) often address our mistakes. If we err one way, we tend to overcompensate in the other direction to ensure that we don't mess up again "just in case." Race is a good example. We treated blacks poorly so it wound us up in a lot of trouble. Thankfully, we're past that (unfortunately there are still those out there who hold prejudices against a person's skin tone—garbage, if you ask me), but so we don't screw up again, we embrace *all* things "different" from us (whites and/or people) so as to not "screw up" again. As noble as that intention may have started out, it's obviously gotten sidetracked and then we're back on the subject of the absence of absolute black and absolute white in society and are instead stuck with a bunch of gray tones for fear of messing up again. Anyone who maintains a view of "absolutes" are then labeled as extremists or fundamentalists (i.e. like many Christians are labeled as) and then we get scolded for not being "open" or "tolerant." As mentioned in my previous letter, tolerance and "letting anything go" has been historically proven to send society on a spiral downward. It's only a matter of time but, like you said, a process we need to go through. I can only help but wonder when we'll "wake up" and realize that how we've been doing things truly isn't the way to go. How bad will it have to get before we slap ourselves on the forehead and go, "Duh! We're idiots and we screwed up!"? Only the future will tell, I suppose.

Anyway, I'm enjoying our talks and look forward to further correspondence. Will you be releasing a *Collected Letters 2005* or was the *2004* edition a one-off thing?

Sincerely,

John Urbancik

February 20, 2006

Dear John:

The other day I finished reading your portion of *The Rise and Fall of Babylon*, *Babylon Rising*. First and foremost, thank you for the entertaining read. What I enjoyed most about it was its—to me—slower pacing as lately I've been reading a bunch of books of the more "whittled down/lots of dialogue/less description/move, move, move" variety. It was a pleasant change to read something with detail and something, which was evident in the tone of the text, written with deep care and heart.

The edition of *The Rise and Fall of Babylon* I had read was the softcover chapbook. A few highlights that I marked to comment on, if for no better reason other than they really entertained me:

Page 8: The image of when the lightning struck and for the briefest of instances Gabriel caught a glimpse of the bones illuminating beneath the soldier's skin. This really jumped out at me and was one of the main images you painted that came up crystal clear in my mind's eye. Well done.

Page 17: The mention of the merchants and buyers parting like the Red Sea as Gabriel sped past with the guards. Whether this was intentional on your part or not, using the words "Red Sea"—the image immediately bringing to mind ancient Biblical days—was a great way to really establish the "time/era" your story took place in and firmly cement it in the reader's head. Kind of a point of reference type of thing.

Page 18: The prisoner heard in Gabriel's mind who spoke of the thousand and one virgins. This is a hint at the way the afterlife is believed to be by Muslims. I'm not sure precisely the exact year your story takes place, but it would be safe to say after 684AD, right? 684AD (I'm pretty sure that was the year) was when Mohammed had come out of the cave and started the Muslim religion. No matter. Just found it interesting.

Page 26: The image of the woman pressing her finger to the side of her chin as if keeping her head in place atop her shoulders. Ha! This reminded me of a school teacher I once had in elementary.

But truly, John, good work. Like I mentioned above, it felt really good to read a more detailed piece of work as, for me, that style of writing is my preference. I'm of the type who would rather get too much information instead of not enough, would rather read a scene in detail than later feel cheated because the author seemed to gloss over it (which happens far too much in the cookie cutter fiction style that plagues bookstore shelves).

I look forward to reading more from you in the future.

All the best,

Jon Klement

March 6, 2006

Dear Jon:

So, what's new in the world of Rush and the Grey Fox? I just signed up for free at RushandtheGreyFox.com for their continuing adventures. I see you have the first two chapters up. I'm eager to hear how things went at that convention you said you were going to back in January. So, how did it go?

As I had mentioned to you earlier, I was to begin work on a superhero project of my own this year. The work has begun and I'm currently sitting at around 10,000 words, so probably about a sixth to the end given how long I estimate the tale to be from the current pace the story is presently unfolding. I'm eager to see how it all turns out and I can see the addiction in bringing one's own superhero creation to the page. I haven't had this much fun creating since I first created my superhero character back in high school. What's his name? You'll have to wait until my formal announcement to find out.

As a point of interest, and since I know you're a follower of Jesus as well, I have the first three in a planned five-part article series up on my blog at http://coscomentertainment.blogspot.com The purpose is posting these articles is not to shove the Gospel down a person's throat but rather one of proclamation. The blog is, of course, not directed at any one person but only toward the person who is reading it, if that makes sense. It's been pressed upon my heart to really share the hardcore reality of the Scriptures and to inform people that this isn't a joke but rather something to take seriously. The Scriptures aren't just some story concocted thousands of years ago, but rather a coherent historical text chronicling God's movement since day one and up to two thousand years ago when John the Revelator was told what to write in the final chapter and to "seal it up." The idea that the Bible is "one big story"—"story" being the operative word—It's impossible. It was written over a long, long time, a few thousand years for starters. Even if a chain of writers "picked up where the other left off," and continued the "story" forward, a) to keep everything straight and as interconnecting in its multiple, multiple layers as it is would be impossible for just one man at a time and b) if, say, for each book of the Bible a team of writers were assigned to "complete the next chapter in the story," they would have had to have an extreme ability to relay information to each other *clearly* on top of keeping consistent with the previous installments and adhering to the layers and reference points (that is the reference points which point to the other books in the Bible) of each book in the Bible's text and c) the editorial team that would have been needed to oversee the project and "keep it all together and flawless in its continuity" would have to have been incredible (not to mention utterly and completely clear in their vision over the course of thousands of years for fear of messing up, so the communication from one generation to the next over great distances would have to have been astounding to say the least). But the idea of an "editing team" doesn't work either because a) no book exists today that is 100% error free (and the Bible is error free), b) any writer will tell you that there are only so many drafts one can do on a manuscript before one runs the risk of over-editing, which then leads to, basically, the disintegration of the story and coherency and flow, and everything written begins to literally fall apart at the seams. Then of course you'd have to account for all the historical evidence that supports the Bible both during the time it was written and the events that happened after (like the destruction of Jerusalem in 70AD which was prophesied by Daniel and was carried out to the letter), and never mind all the supernatural things that have occurred prior and up to this present day and age that only happen when the Bible is followed to the letter. I could ramble on for pages on the aforementioned points alone never mind the countless others that support the Bible as authentic, so I'll leave it here for now.

Anyway, just checking in to see what's new in your neck of the woods. Talk to you later.

Sincerely,

Dave Sim

March 8, 2006

Dear Dave:

Thanks for your recent letter, the latest having covered a lot of ground. I'll just go through yours in order and do a point-by-point/section-by-section reply in the interest of staying organized.

My rate for copyediting is 1 cent US per word and for a Canadian client it's still 1 cent US per word but then come invoice day, whatever the US total is, it is exchanged at that day's current exchange rate to arrive at the Canadian dollar value of the total. Since the Canadian dollar is doing well these days (lately we've been hovering around 1.11-1.13 on the exchange), it's not too big of a deal. If this was a few years ago where our dollar stunk and the exchange averaged at around 1.65, then unfortunately for the Canadian client, the service would cost them more.

The comment about "by Dave Sim as told to so-and-so," I see where you're coming from. I don't believe it's an editor's job—copyeditor or just proofreader—to rewrite anything or "redo" anything. The job is to point out to the author where he/she messed up regarding continuity, grammar, spelling, etc. Sure, an editor corrects words or puts question marks beside word choices (especially ones that don't fit the context of any given statement), but it'd have to be a super heavy "redo" for them to have any righteous claim to a joint byline. That, and any suggestion/correction an editor makes, the author can say no to especially if they've hired someone on a freelance basis to go over the manuscript. There's always a written agreement, too, that so-and-so was hired for such-and-such a service, he/she is to be paid X amount for said service and that's where the relationship ends.

I liked your idea of just stepping back from all this "creative" stuff and getting a McJob. Trust me, I hear you. I've toyed with that idea too and instead of being glued to my work station for 10-12 hours a day, it'd be nice to do my 8 hours and not worry about work until the next block of 8 hours rolled around. Ah, the price we pay for following our dreams and seeing our goals through. And, in truth, I wouldn't trade this job for anything. Well, maybe being an action star.

You haven't sent me a copy of the *Cerebus Guide to Self-publishing*, but it's okay; I already have a copy (see my first letter to you). Thanks for the offer, though.

So on to the "meat" of our correspondence: our foray into the world of the gray stuff. You had used abortion as an example in your comments. After I first read it, I quickly saw that such a topic could open a door into a discussion on one's morals and religious beliefs (yours, mine, whoever's). But I'll try to keep that separate for now as best I can because, since you and I are dealing in the medium of letter writing, I'll attempt to keep things simple instead of sending you a 10-page letters each mailing and vice versa (though, of course, I'm not opposed to long letters written and sent by either one of us). So in summation, if I understood your point correctly, we take an issue like abortion, create a "spectrum of extremes"—so Abortion Yes on one end and Abortion No on the other—and then with our pens draw up lines where each line is connected to a "reason" for the abortion and depending where that line is on the spectrum, it would either be closer to Abortion Yes or Abortion No. Or am I making it too complicated? Before delving into that, I'm not sure if the jurisdictional approach to abortion (or the prison terms for a certain crime or whatnot) would work in that if I live in the north end of town and want an abortion but in my jurisdiction abortion is illegal, what would stop me from going to the south end, where it is allowed, to get it done? Unless, of course, that the jurisdiction you live in is the one you *have to* adhere to lest you face a fine or jail and even if you went to the south end they wouldn't perform the procedure for you because you would be required to produce two pieces of ID that state your address and what jurisdiction you're in. You're from the north, tough beans, buddy!

The spectrum approach is an interesting one, but by allowing different nuances to see where upon it you fall, are we not then opening up the door to more gray stuff? If one end is white, the other black, the stuff in between has to be varying shades of gray. For the record, I'm pro-life (which we can always get into a discussion on at a different time) as murder's murder no matter which way you slice it. Even when you kill someone in self-defense, you've still killed them. And depending how you look at it, abortion is a form of self-defense as the female is "saving" herself from something—fill-in-the-blank, here. But then what of our incest victims or our rape victims or our twelve-year-old teens who were taken advantage of by Daddy's friend and are now with a thirty-year-old's child? Wherever that situation(s) falls on the spectrum, should they be allowed to end a life if either a) it's just a cluster of cells in the womb so by ending it you're denying it the right to develop into a child and live or b) it's a maturing fetus that's four months into development but then you're disallowing his/her birth? I think the real question is: where are we getting our laws from and what are we basing them on? This, of course, could sidetrack us into the religious arena so I'm trying to avoid that for now, but it does make one wonder from where/when we got our laws and who made them. The nuances thing could work but it would have to be on a very tight and, dare I say, rigid platform without room for leniency, because the thing with nuances is, in the context we are talking about here, each circumstance is different—especially when dealing with rape or incest (i.e. was the defendant coerced into the intercourse? Was it forced? Did they go into it willingly but then things got out of hand and so it was rape? etc.)—it opens the doors to a plethora of nuances and thickens the gray area. In Winnipeg alone, there are around 700,000 people and over half are women, so for the sake of discussion, if all the women in Winnipeg ended up being either rape or incest victims, we're dealing with a possible 350,000+ unique circumstances that each carry nuances of their own. I know from this and from my previous letters to you that my personal desire to see the restoration or black and white in society may come off as if I want to live in a dictatorship or under a similar type of government. That's not the case but I thought I should clarify that just in case. My main issue would be to challenge those "in charge" (and I use the term loosely) and Mr. Everyday Joe to take a real hard and objective look at how things are run, how we're living our lives and, further, *why* we are heading down the road of "anything goes." Which then kind of takes us back to the "each circumstance is different so yields a unique outcome" argument, the "we're all different and unique so what I view as wrong might not be what you view as wrong" thing, which then takes us back again to *why* we think/feel the way we do. We only have three possible scenarios of outcome if two disagreeing people were to find out why they thought something: either I would be wrong, you would be right, or I would be right and you would be wrong, or we're both wrong. The thing of it is, we can't both be right when you're dealing with yes or no, true or fals, up or down, left or right, black or white issues (which most issues are if we dare to trim away all the "fat" that we've layered around the things of everyday life). But those "outcomes," referring to the aforementioned "each circumstance is different so yields a unique outcome," each yield a different *specific* result but on a broader scale. For the sake of example, let's take murder. Whether I killed someone intentionally, killed them in self-defense, or abetted a murder, they all resulted in the *specific* outcome of someone's death. Then the real question is to what degree should I be held accountable? Dare I say fully? Regardless of the original intention or circumstance, the way it panned out resulted in the loss of life. *I'm* responsible for that loss of life because of my actions. I was involved therefore I am responsible. Then what of my punishment? Should it be the same as that if I went out and killed someone I disliked or if I instead shot you because you had a gun aimed at my head? This is why other evidence comes into play when they sentence someone: was it premeditated? Was it done out of malice or out of defense? As a thought, how about a set penalty for a crime that can be added to based upon the "other crimes" perpetrated at the time of said crime? Example, the penalty for murder is ten years in the pen regardless of circumstance. If I pre-planned the murder, another five years. Was it one victim or two? If it's one and it was intentional, I get put away for 15 years. If it's two people, then I go away for 30 and/or a sentence where the death of each person on your deathlist has to be paid for in increments of, say, 5 years. That's not to say a person's life is only worth 5 year's in the pen—as obviously the victim's family would no doubt like to see you hanged or put away for good—but the point would be to set a set penalty for whatever crime. I'm not a lawyer, a cop nor politician nor will I pretend to know the law inside out and backwards. Maybe this approach is far too simple. But then again, maybe it isn't.

Moving on...

I'm pleased to hear you possibly doing future *Collected Letters* editions. I'm still reading the first one. I admit to taking a break from it as I just dove in to and completed a 12-book fiction series so wanted to take the time to read those. But I'll be getting back to your book any day now. As a suggestion—and also from the point of view as a consumer/reader—please consider making them at least 200 pages long, 250 being ideal, if/when you release more. From the consumer's point of view, it's the whole bang for your buck thing. The current *2004* edition is printed at 8.5" x 11", right? If you decided to pursue POD for it, and utilize the Lightning Source option I suggested, as a FYI, to POD print at anything larger than 6.14" x 9.21" it increases your per unit cost (I believe that's the top size before it costs more though I don't have my notes in front of me; I know there is a page size limit before increase though). A suggestion might be—depending on how much material you have—to publish each volume as a quarterly publication, where, say, Jan-Mar '05 would be in one book, Apr-Jun '05 in another and so forth. Of course each book would be slightly bigger or smaller than the previous based on the volume of mail you received. Then if you took your reply letters and formatted them at, say, 5.5" x 8.5" or 6" x 9", to fill that 200-250 pages wouldn't be a problem and you'd save a little on your per unit print cost. As an idea, too, I wonder if adding even a three-page Cerebus story or one-panel/page Cerebus gag would get readers from the regular storyline to pick up the *Letters* book(s) because of the included art?

The other day I thought, "Gee, I wonder if Dave has ever thought about crossing over into the electronic publishing business either through Aardvark-Vanaheim or via a partnership with another firm?" I'm referring to eBooks. Though I don't see them ever replacing an old-fashioned print book, they do open the doors to readers who prefer the electronic reading format. There's 10+ different e-formats ranging from a simple PDF file you can read on your computer screen to a format where you can download the text into a handheld device that's akin to a Tricorder and you can tote it around like a regular print book. I had thought, "I wonder if Dave has considered doing this for either his text-based *Collected Letters* volume(s) or even for the *Cerebus* trades?" Obviously the goal with any creator is to share his/her work with as many folks as possible. As a thought, putting the *Cerebus* trades into e-format might be beneficial to the sales of your phonebook volumes. Your phonebooks retail for about $25-30 Canadian. Well, if I'm new to Cerebus and his world or just have a partial interest in it, I might not be willing to spend the $25-30 for the book. However, I might be willing to spend $10 for the eBook edition (eBooks typically retail for less than the print version by about half). If I liked what I read/saw in the e-version, I might get the next volume in print and/or replace my e-version by shelling out for the print version (I know of some people who do this for novels). EBooks are a good way for people to try out authors they've never heard of or are just interested in but are unsure if that author can deliver the same wallop every outing like, say, Stephen King or Alan Moore. Anyway, it's just a thought, Dave, but since eBooks require zero maintenance save the initial work to format them, the profits yielded might be a nice additional income during your retirement. Passive income. I believe Gerhard has a site set up for auctioning off some original art, right? If you pursued the "e-option," he could put up some links on there as to where online readers can purchase the e-versions of *Cerebus*, make an announcement to the Yahoos, send out a press release online, and all the rest.

Anyway, I've rattled on a little longer than I originally estimated. I hope all is well with you. I look forward to your reply.

Sincerely,

Scott Hintz

March 10, 2006

Dear Scott:

Thanks for writing. Glad to hear you enjoy my work. Which one(s) have you read?

I'd be more than happy to do a link exchange with you. I'll pass on your info to my webmaster to implement during the next site update.

Thanks again.

Best,

Brian Keene

March 11, 2006

Dear Brian:

I have read your half of *The Rise and Fall of Babylon, Babylon Falling.* I read the softcover chapbook edition.

Some favorite parts:

Pg. 10 – Sanchez wishing God would send them a couple of Chinooks to fly them out of there. Found this funny whether you meant it to be a joke or not. I found it amusing because God could have easily willed in to being a couple of Chinooks to save the day.

Pg. 15 – The old man stating they don't read the Koran but something much older. My first thought was the Bible since, as far as I'm aware, Biblical writings are among the earliest save for maybe caveman paintings. I'm referring to the Torah, of course. But I was proven wrong as to what the old fella was referring to was the *Daemonolateria* (see comment below).

Pg. 17 – When Williams was informed his eyes were going to be taken. Just the pacing of this was awesome because when you said Williams didn't scream and the others screamed for him, it brought on a flood of dread, something so bad that the guy it was going to be done to was speechless, something so bad that his friends all screamed at the very thought of what was about to happen. One would think that if you were caught in that position with your buds, it would be the other way around.

For the *Daemonolateria* book, you had me convinced it was a real book. I actually went to Amazon.ca to see if it was—to see if you were making it up or not—but I guess not. Good job on fooling me. I suppose it's better that it was a fake anyway as we have enough of those kinds of books in the real world. No sense adding one more. The reason I say that is bizarre and dangerous things tend to happen when one gets involved in summoning things that are off limits. I have a friend who messed around with the *Necronomicon* before giving his life to Christ and he recounted me the details of what happened. Scary stuff. This, of course, could spark an entire dialogue on the unseen realm. Fascinating stuff though one to be approached with healthy caution. The idea is balance ala how C.S. Lewis put it, basically stating that to be obsessed with the devil and the evil spirits in the world of the unseen is pure folly, but to ignore them completely is also equally dangerous.

Thanks for the great read, Brian.

On a bit of a down note, I had informed you in my previous letter that Indigo.ca was to be shipping me a copy of *The Rising*. I got an email a couple of weeks back (roughly) stating that they couldn't get their hands on a copy. As per your blog you said it was nearly out of print. Is a third printing going to happen?

Thanks again.

Sincerely,

Stephen King

March 15, 2006

Dear Stephen:

I can't begin to tell you how many times I thought of the perfect opening for a letter to you. And I can't begin to tell you how many times that perfect opening escaped me. Rest assured, this is not a fan letter although I do admire your work. And I promise this isn't a letter of praises although I do think you're one heck of a writer.

But all joking aside, this is a letter of gratitude, and though this is probably the umpteenth letter of this sort you've received, please know that I mean every word.

Thank you for your inspiration over the years even though you and I have never met, and up until this moment you have never heard of me. Back while dabbling in 2D animation school, I was living in a ratty apartment and one night I caught *Fear, Fame and Fortune* on A&E. After watching it, the seed was planted to, as it turned out, soon put my own stories to paper. What inspired me about the program wasn't anything to do with the rags-to-riches angle, but rather the gung ho and deep, deep drive to get one's stories out of their head and into some tangible form. And what a better way to do that than to write a book. I admit to several false starts and it wasn't until a series of four or five short stories—meant to be linked together—came out did I realize I had the prologue to my first novel. More on that in a second. But while I was working on my story, I kept thinking about that biography, the idea that entire worlds exist in a writer's mind and the absolute truth that they do not need to stay there.

What's inspired me most about your work is the depth in which you tell your stories and the density of your characters. Even your characters who have all of a page's worth of "screen time" are just as real as those of the main cast. The one that really got me good was *Bag of Bones.* I had read it sometime in 2000 (I think), while working on my first novel, *A Stranger Dead* (encl.). I pass a copy of the novel on to you to use as you will. Though I stand by the *story*—that is what it's about and what happens event-wise throughout the tale—110%, I'll tell you straight up that the writing is terrible. I plan on revising it and re-publishing someday after a thorough clean up. How did it get published if it was so terrible? It was done through a subsidy press. Yes, I got desperate. I won't bore you with the details but in the end, I came out on top regarding lessons learned. I enclose the novel with this letter because it was my first novel, my first baby, and though it has more warts than an ugly step-sister, it's still special simply because it was the first, and I'd like you to have a copy. (Besides, your name appears on the acknowledgements page anyway.)

As a quick sidebar, your honest-to-God respect and surrender to *story* parallels my own. A story is a living, breathing thing, something that *must* be adhered to at all times. I've never been able to understand writers who use outlines or who plot an entire story before actually writing it. To me, that's putting the story in a box, giving it limits before the creating of it is complete. For any story of merit—"merit" in this instance referring to a story of truth and honesty (for writing *is* honesty)—the writer must surrender his/herself to the story, let the story flow through them, steer them, and go with it wherever it pleases. Even during the rewrite stage as you and I tweak our tales, we're still listening to the story, discarding the fluff, adding/revealing the gold (though this stage is arguably a paradox), so that, when all is said and done, the story is presented *as it is* in its purest form. Straight up truth.

But things have changed since I started and the benchmark for quality fiction that you have set is one I try to reach with every sitting at the keyboard. I still have a long way to go, but also enclosed is my latest novel, *The Way of the Fog,* which was published as a limited edition. As of this writing I'm working on selling the mass market rights to it. In the end, of course, only time—and New York—will tell what happens with the tale. It has received endorsements from such notables as Piers Anthony and Douglas Clegg, so I figure it can't be all that bad and I must have made some progress. You've done well in entertaining me with your stories so please consider *The Way of the Fog* my attempt at doing the same. Just for the sake of "clearing the air," please note the book is *not* enclosed for reasons of endorsement or comment or anything. As said, you've given me several ripping yarns; it's the least I could do in return. I just sincerely want to say thanks for everything. (I, of course, wouldn't be opposed to hearing from you should you be inspired to drop me a note/line.)

Though I'd like to go on for pages, I also realize you have projects on the go and other things happening so I'll leave you for now. Perhaps one day our paths will cross at a convention or a gathering of some sort, and maybe then we'll talk more in detail.

But truthfully, Stephen, thanks for the inspiration, for the entertainment, and though we've never met, for being approachable and down to earth. In short, *On Writing* hit me hard because I saw a lot of myself in the trials you went through before you got where you are today, and reading that book was like sitting down across from you at a coffee shop, talking the biz and, more importantly, talking stories. Thanks again.

Your friend on the page,

Eric M. Cooper

March 24, 2006

Dear Eric:

How are things? I'm writing to see how the new *Knight Seeker* novel is coming along? I was thinking about the character the other day and am curious when I might see him next?

I'm also writing to advise you that I maintain a weekly blog called *Coscomment*, and this week's entry might interest you as it deals with independent superhero creations. The URL is http://coscomentertainment.blogspot.com

I hope all is well with you. Take care.

Sincerely,

Frank Creed

March 27, 2006

Dear Frank:

Thanks for purchasing *Book Marketing for the Financially-challenged Author.* I'll ship it promptly. The book, of course, isn't a "how to" on self-pubbing or anything. Just basically a book on marketing ideas that, all told, cost about the cost of a meal. I understand most authors are poor so why spend money on promo when you don't have to?

Before I answer your question, I want to make it clear—in the interest of avoiding any possible confusion—that I'm not a self-publishing guru nor as wildly successful as Dan Poynter. However, I stand by self-publishing as an equivalent to small press publishing (or possibly bigger) *as long as it's done properly*. And that last part is key. There are self-publishers, the thousands and thousands of them, who have NOT done it properly, hence the stigma associated with self-publishing one's work. Straight up and honest, it's an uphill battle straight through. But it does yield its rewards, an example being that as of this writing, a huge door has been opened up to me in the traditional publishing world and, God willing, it'll come to full fruition so I can spread the Message through my work.

That part out of the way, your question about genre jumping. If you're referring to, say, writing a romance book then a fantasy title then a horror title, etc., from a marketing standpoint, and for an unknown writer, it can cause some issues, but to me, that's all dependent on how you play your cards. Yet even the big boys in New York know it can cause some problems so that's why they get even some of their top name writers to write under a pseudonym even if that pseudonym is widely known (i.e. Nora Roberts who also writes under J.D. Robb). I did the same when I released my love story, *April*. Since it was a story unlike my other work (which consists of horror/supernatural fiction and fantasy), I chose to release it under the name Peter Fox (though I made no secret about this). What this did was notify those who read me as A.P. Fuchs that this book was not a standard A.P. Fuchs offering, but something completely different. If I had released it under A.P. Fuchs and even after folks read the synopsis, they still might have been counting on a story with a supernatural edge, of which this love story had none of. That has been my only experience on the matter. My non-fiction work has all been released under A.P. Fuchs and I plan on doing the same with a couple non-fiction titles I'll be releasing next year. If I do another love story, it'll be under Peter Fox again. Fortunately for myself, my "genre" is speculative fiction, which consists of mainly three topics: horror, sci-fi and fantasy, so I've got my bases covered "genre-wise." Only my latest fantasy, *The Way of the Fog*, is blatantly Christian, where as my horror stuff is supernatural in nature and only hints at a Christian background, but they're definitely secular. I wish I could be of further assistance on this but perhaps what was said here might be enough to go on as a starting point.

Like I tell anyone considering self-publishing: do your research, go slow, and go in to it knowing that it's not easy and it takes time and work and a thick skin.

I look forward to corresponding with you further.

God bless you.

Best,

Piers Anthony

April 3, 2006

Dear Piers:

Thank you very much again for taking the time to read my novel, *The Way of the Fog.* And thank you, as well, for your kind words about it in your April newsletter. Your review made me smile.

Aside from your great review of my book, what touched me about your newsletter was your comment about helping newer writers via "boost blurbs." This approachable attitude and desire to help the "newbie" is truly commendable, so my hat's off to you. Some popular writers are very approachable and some, when success comes their way, suddenly act like they're the greatest gift to the medium and don't touch newer writers or even associate with them. What I find ironic about that is they're turning away the very thing they once were—new writers. Again, good form on your part for reaching out to those of us lower on the bookselling chain.

I hope all is well with you and I look forward to your future columns.

Sincerely,

Todd Michael Greene

May 10, 2006

Dear Todd:

Thanks for contacting me. I'm glad to hear you're currently on the quest to be published. I'd be more than happy to keep in touch with you in this regard. As well, I always find it helpful to keep in touch with fellow Christians.

Thanks for the links as well.

Best,

Steven Jorgenson

May 18, 2006

Dear Steven:

Thanks for writing. What I meant by *The Way of the Fog* being 235k, is that the book is approx. 235,000 words long (so roughly the length of 3 normal-sized novels). It's my longest work to date. Book Two is about a third completed at 80k as of this writing. I'll be resuming work on it come July once I finish a sci-fi project I'm currently working on.

Yes, I have kicked myself for dinging a book. When I used to have a day job, I'd read on the bus on the way to work. For a long while I was a member of a book club so most of my books are in hardcover (you can get them fairly cheap in Canadian book clubs for anywhere between $14-16). I always take the dust jacket off when reading a hardcover and so I traveled with the book without it. I kept it in my backpack and, between pulling it out and plopping it back in, I damaged the cardboard of Robert Jordan's *The Wheel of Time* Book Four pretty good. I'm the kind of guy who likes his books in pristine condition, if it can be helped. So, yeah, I definitely hear where you're coming from.

Thank you for taking a chance on *The Way of the Fog*, by the way. It is very much appreciated as I'm fully aware, compared to other authors out there, I'm an unknown so every time I hear from a reader who has a copy of my work, it makes me feel good. I truly hope you're enjoying the tale and, once done, are eager to see what happens next.

Talk to you later.

Best,

Dave Sim

June 4, 2006

Dear Dave:

This is the second time I've apologized to you for my tardy reply. I got your letter beginning of April but with tax season demands, looming deadlines and my recent business trip to Florida (of which I just returned from), I wasn't able to write to you. Have you been to Florida? Aside from the business aspect of my trip, I was also there for pleasure. The major highlight was Universal Studios, namely Islands of Adventure featuring a plethora of Marvel characters and, best of all, an incredible (or should I say *amazing*) Spider-man ride. You might enjoy something like that if you haven't done so already.

So, on to our discussion.

Regarding objective standards for continuity in any given manuscript, there has to be some measure of which to adhere to. What I mean is basic commonsense "rules" that apply to any story. I may have mentioned it before as an example, maybe not, but one would be your main character's hair color should remain the same throughout the entire book unless you specifically state he/she took the time to dye their hair. Or, you can't have one guy start off as African American (Canadian?) and then turn Caucasian halfway through. Or if you make it clear Character Joe needs to get to Hotel A to solve his crime but then have him go to 7-11 to solve it there without mentioning why 7-11 was a suitable substitute or ever mentioning Hotel A again, it'll cause a problem. That's the continuity stuff I was referring to. Just basic things.

On the abortion issue, in short, whatever the jurisdictional rules are regarding having an abortion, they would need to apply to *all* jurisdictions in the province otherwise it would open doors to the gray issues again, which could lead us right back to where we started from. Your rules in Kitchener-Centre are the most rigid I've heard of, and of which I side with. (Though on a personal note I'm against abortion regardless of the circumstance leading up to it; after all, adoption once the baby is born is a possibility.) To be frank, I don't know if we'll be able to continue this "debate" based on that because killing is killing no matter which way you slice it. I don't think I'm trying to reclaim the moral high ground (I freely admit I'm far from perfect) in comparing abortion to murder or drawing lines between the two. It's more just me calling a spade a spade. Whether it's abortion or the intentional pulling of a trigger, the result is the same: loss of life. One has taken the initiative to deny a human being their existence whether just a baby or a full grown person. Who are we to decide who lives and who dies? Who or what gives us that power? My original intent in writing you was not to get into any *heated* debate (I don't think we're at that point at present) but if this abortion discussion will take us down that road, then I politely withdraw from it and we can move on to something else. So that said, in summary, yeah, the jurisdictional approach would be best provided all jurisdictions are on the same page. I like the idea that if you had sex, had an unwanted pregnancy, now it's *your* problem not society's. That I agree with because, to me, it seems far too many folks (at least here in Winnipeg) dump their issues on "society" versus taking responsibility for them themselves. And that's one of the things it really comes down to in the end when it comes to this thing called life: taking responsibility for one's actions. Too many people are passing the buck and pointing fingers instead of raising their hand and saying, "Yup, that was me and here's what I'm going to do to fix it."

The idea for the *Cerebus* e-volumes was just that—an idea.

Opening the book of another discussion, I know the story of how *Cerebus* came to be so I won't ask you to repeat it. However, I was wondering what prompted you to self-publish it instead of trying to sell a publishing firm on the idea? I always enjoy hearing the motives behind a self-publisher's ventures. For myself, it was the age-old thing of being unable to sell my first manuscript, which led to my originally being duped by a vanity press. But after that, I took control, started the company and went from there. Since then I've found the experience rewarding despite some of the more trying days. The knowledge and experience gained is something you can't buy nor learn from reading a how-to book on the subject.

Thank you for taking the time to reply to my letters. It's always good to find a reply from you waiting in my mailbox.

I wish you all the best, Dave. I look forward to your reply.

Sincerely,

Jeff Davis

June 20, 2006

Dear Jeff:

Thanks for the comment on the *Coscomment* entry, "Politcal Uncorrectness." It was just one of those things that had to be said. As mentioned in the article/entry, we live in such a wishy-washy society when it comes to what is right and what is wrong. And, unfortunately, if we continue down that path, it *will* lead to our undoing. I'm not sure how big into prophecy you are, but you might be aware that in the last days immorality will be on the rise and people will become more and more lovers of themselves instead of God. If you take a moment and look around, that's exactly what is happening, more so today than ever before in human history. God seems to be on the back burner for most. And since we're told we're either hot or cold, there isn't any room for being luke warm. One or the other, yes or no. Left or right, black or white. Pick one.

Thanks again for your comment. Feel free to pass around the link to the entry to any you feel might benefit from it.

Blessings,

Richard Pulfer

June 23, 2006

Dear Richard:

Thank you for your email. I'll answer your questions as best as I can.

In order:

To get your book into the hands of major published writers for a chance at a blurb, truthfully, it is just a matter of asking them. Long ago, when I first started seeking blurbs, I reconciled myself to approach the process with a "The worst they could do is say no" kind of attitude. And in truth, that's really the worst that could happen in any scenario and not just when it comes to asking for a blurb. A "no" may not be want you want to hear, but realistically, the world won't end if that's what you're told. Also note that if whomever you ask does agree to read your material, that doesn't obligate them to blurb it if they dislike your book for whatever reason. I always inform the person of that up front so they don't feel pressured. After all, *they're* the ones doing you the favor. I also suggest to be 110% professional in your letter to them (keep it brief) and not once come across as a whiny fan. I'm sure you know this but it doesn't hurt to have a reminder because, as is often the case when starting out in this business, most writers *are* whiny fans and kiss the other author's butt in order to gain favor. Authors aren't stupid and they see right through this.

Regarding consignment, interestingly enough, the entire book industry functions on consignment (albeit a more complicated version of it), but in the scale you're asking about, the process is very simple.

Step One: Pick a bookstore you wish for your book to appear in (this is assuming you don't have any distribution or wholesale channels for your project).

Step Two: Call them up and ask to speak to whoever is in charge of consigned books.

Step Three: Inform Mr./Ms. Consignment of your project (i.e. who you are and what your book is about) and see if they're willing to take on some copies. As to the quantity, this varies from store to store. In my experience it's been as little as two to as much as ten, in one shot.

Step Four: If they're interested, arrange a time to meet with them. Bring your books down and go over the agreement. If they're not interested, thank them anyway and move on to the next store.

Step Five: Repeat for all stores you wish to carry your book.

In summary, consignment, generally, is based on the following principles and I'd personally be leery of anything that strays from this. They are:

- Bookstore takes book(s) without any up front payment to you.
- Bookstore always takes your book at a discount (X% off cover price; in Canada it's 40-45% and in the US, don't quote me, but I think it's around 40% as well, perhaps less).

- If your books sell, you get paid the discounted price multiplied by however many copies sold.
- If your books don't sell, you come and pick them up and it's as if it never happened.

As a friendly warning, consigned agreements usually state the store can return the books to you in ANY condition. I always make a point of informing whoever I'm dealing with that they have to be in good, re-sellable condition so I can at least get rid of them via the direct market. No sense having a bunch of dinged up paperbacks cluttering up your office.

That's basically it. Shelf life is the store's decision and, if they sell out, if they end up getting more from you. Again, that's for consignment. As the "supplier" of your books, assuming you have your own company, you can also inform the stores of your sales policy and if your books are returnable or not. But that's a whole other thing to talk about.

From what I know of US booksellers, as that's where I assume you're from, the big chains are reluctant to get in books from self-publishers for numerous reasons, the big one being the stigma of quality. Some of the big chains have hard-as-stone policies on saying no to ALL self-publishers, whereas others can be persuaded provided you're charming and show them how *they* can benefit from your book financially. And that's the real issue. It's all about the money in this business whether one agrees with that or not. All I can say is that it doesn't hurt to ask. The worst they can do is say no, right? Indy stores are usually a better bet for unloading your books. If your book is subsidy published (i.e. you paid a fee for a service from a "publisher," they'll automatically say no. Lulu.com falls under this category as well).

Have I had success in the consignment arena? Yes. My books have been/are on shelves all over the city and folks have purchased them from those stores and I've been paid for them. I measure my success not so much on the numbers side of things

(I'm not Stephen King), but rather on the grounds of, "Are people reading my books and are they selling beyond the default of friends and family?" If I can answer yes to that question, then I consider it a success. And since I can say yes to that question, I consider myself successful. On the dollars and cents side of things, what I make off a project is comparable to those who get published by an advance-paying small-to-medium-sized press.

There's a whole lot more to promoting than consignment (which I'm sure you know). As a blatant solicitation to you, I have a book called *Book Marketing for the Financially-challenged Author* which covers all sorts of promotion ideas that can be executed by the "starving artist." I have copies available if you're interested.

I hope the above has helped you, Richard.

Thanks.

Best,

Todd Michael Greene

June 25, 2006

Dear Todd:

Thanks for linking to APFuchs.com, Coscom Entertainment and *Coscomment*. It is much appreciated. I'll pass a note onto my webmaster to include a link to your site on my own the next time I update.

Thanks again.

Sincerely,

Darryl Sloan

July 3, 2006

Dear Darryl:

Thanks for your note and for sharing your own experience akin to *Coscomment*'s "Those Bursts of Color." I have to agree with you that it was a spiritual attack by the enemy. I've been slugging it out with him big time starting roughly three weeks ago. (He first led me to momentarily believe I had committed the unpardonable sin; let me tell you, that was the most terrifying moment of my life. Right now he's still planting doubts in my head that I'm redeemed in Christ so I'm clinging to the Lord more than ever these days.) The truth is, too, that one of the devil's major end-times tactics is to wear out the saints (see Daniel 7:25). I stumbled upon this little nugget of truth the other day while reading *Enjoying Everyday Life*, a monthly magazine put out by Joyce Meyer Ministries. I'm convinced God led me to the article as one of His many ways of speaking to me (He has a knack for speaking to me right when I need to hear something from Him the most. He truly is faithful, just like His Word says He is). But let that also be a "heads up" to you regarding what the devil might throw your (or any believer's) way. I'm one of those folks who are of the mindset that this is the final generation before the Second Coming. I can take up pages upon pages of why I think so—the proof these days is overwhelming—but in short, we're in the generation of the fig tree (see Matthew 24) and the fig tree began blooming in 1948 when Israel was reborn as a nation. The point is, we believers are up against some hard times until we're caught up in the air to meet Jesus. However, the victory is His (though at times it's hard to remember that). Your email was a friendly reminder of what it was I really felt the other day and who was attacking me. Thanks. It truly is appreciated.

Best,

Susan Kirkland

July 5, 2006

Dear Susan:

Thanks for your note. I looked into the publishing company you said you were going to self-publish your book through by going to their website. I went under the "services" section and didn't find any pricing. However, you said it was comparable to other "services" out there so this leads me to assume you're not truly self-publishing your work but rather subsidy-publishing it. By definition, a true self-publisher is one who publishes his/her own books under his/her own company and absorbs all costs for editing, interior design, printing, cover design, distribution and marketing, etc. A subsidy-publisher is one who pays a place like Author House or Iuniverse a "fee" to "publish" their book and only makes a small royalty off of it (usually 10-20% Net or so). I wrote an article for *Horrorworld* on the subject called, "Shaking Hands with the Devil." The thrust of the article was a wake-up call to those wishing to subsidy publish and actually come out on top financially. The truth is, this is impossible unless you have a massive market waiting and even then, what you'd make would be fairly minimal. A brief excerpt from the article:

"On average, these companies charge anywhere from $400-$800+ to "publish" your book. Pretend it ends up costing you only $400. On average, these companies pay out only a 20% Net royalty, typically defined as book cover cost less any wholesale distributor discounts less per-unit print cost of the book. For this example, let's take the average cost of a self-published book, which would be about $15 for a 250-page paperback novel. Using the above formula, $15—40% industry standard discount—$5 (average) per unit print cost = $4 (Net). 20% of $4 is 80 cents. For you to merely break even on your investment if you paired with a subsidy print-on-demand "publisher," you will need to sell

500 copies of your novel never mind being compensated for the thousands of hours it took you to write it and polish it. Can you sell 500 copies of your book by marketing it yourself, which you have to do with these outfits? And this is best case scenario, mind you, despite what most authors actually pay to these places. Think about it."

Again, I don't know much about the company you've chosen or what your fee is so the above is meant as a FYI and a "Be Careful" notice. They may be a great company but if you're not going to make anything off your book, why bother? That's why when someone tells me they want to self-publish for whatever reason, I suggest they either a) forget it and go traditional or b) truly self-publish themselves and not pay a service.

The choice is yours. I hope the above was of some help.

Thanks again for writing.

Sincerely,

Dave Sim

July 10, 2006

Dear Dave:

Taking a breather and a step back, in short, yeah, there are different issues in society that do fluctuate (like your Canada in Afghanistan example) and those which do not (like abortion). We're faced with something that no matter what you choose (i.e. what "rule" is passed), someone is going to be unhappy. Ah, the wonderful world of politics. If I read your reply correctly, a summary would be to basically reach a compromise of some sort amongst the masses on 50-50 issues. It may not float everyone's boat but it's the best we got and all other alternatives are substandard in that regard. The only thing I can think of to say is that a compromise would be a "best case" scenario or an *ideal.* My only concern (or anybody's concern, for that matter) would then be to ask if the "compromise" is the right decision (meaning was it truly right in the purest sense of the word or was it either not-right but something else, or absolutely wrong). And I think that's the real issue when dealing with such sticky subjects. The old saying of, "What I think is right is not necessarily what you think is right" and vice versa, comes to mind. And that's what I meant right from the get-go about the "fluff" of society, or the *gray* stuff as we've been calling it. Either something is white (right) or something is gray (not-right) or black (wrong), but either way, the latter two aren't white. It's basically the quest for truth in the end on how things really and truly are, what things are really and truly right, and what things are really and truly wrong. So then the shift/goal would be to ask how we can discover what is the right course of action and what is the wrong one. And answering that is a huge topic on its own, depending if you're talking to a "religious" person or a "secular" person. And even if we did present a way that proved "this is right" or "this is wrong," it's still up to that individual to accept it or not. The only danger in a person not accepting a proven point would be them putting themselves in a position of denial and/or self-delusion on *how things really are.* Either something is or it isn't. It can't be both. But in the world we live in? Yes, a compromise would be the best we could do and the only *sensible* thing we could do.

Thanks for answering the question on your decision to self-publish. I'm of the same mind in that I'd rather get my stuff out there on a regular basis than have it sit in a drawer or make its way through the mail from one publication to another on submission. And by getting it done on my own, it's opened up doors for me that wouldn't have been opened had I played the "traditional" writer's game of writing, submitting, waiting, writing, submitting, waiting, and so forth.

Sincerely,

Nick Cato

July 22, 2006

Dear Nick:

Thanks for passing your essay on to me for feedback. I found it quite interesting and *bang on* on a lot of points. The one that really jumped out at me was that the world applies the misdeeds of "Christian" men who condemn and accuse people instead of loving them. And then it's that "view" of Christianity which steers the lost away. You're example of the "Rev." Phelps was perfect.

I will, however, disagree with you on one point in your essay, but purely based on your wording. It was on page 5 where you state Jesus does not hate anyone but does hate sin. I would personally clarify that point, namely the "doesn't hate anyone" just so it's clear that just because He doesn't hate you, it doesn't mean sin won't go unpunished if there's no repentance. Yes, He most definitely hates the sin. But regarding loving the sinner—meaning in this context the unsaved—when we were not saved, we were counted as God's enemies (Rom. 5: 9-11), we were children of wrath (Eph. 2:3) and doomed to destruction. So true that God so loved the world that He gave His Son to reconcile all things to Him, but come the separating of the sheep and the goats at the Second Coming, justice will be meted out and His love won't save the unsaved from hell as by then it'll be too late because they had their chance and ended up rejecting Him. Perhaps use the phrase, "Jesus doesn't 'hate' anyone, but does ask they take responsibility for their actions," or something.

I took the liberty of correcting a few things word-wise that jumped out at me as I read it. (All of two things, actually; changes attached to this letter.)

But other than that, good work. Balance is key in this walk called life. The only danger with balancing being a Christian living in the *world* is that we must always be sure we never fall in to the trap of being lukewarm for Christ, but always remain *for* Him in all we do.

See you at the Wedding Feast, but until then, keep in touch online.

In His service,

Richard Pulfer

July 22, 2006

Dear Richard:

Thanks for sending me the third issue of *Coffee Break for Writers* back on July 5. I'm glad the info I gave you came in handy. And thanks for your interest in grabbing your own copy of *Book Marketing for the Financially-challenged Author.*

To answer your questions in your email dated July 21, 2006:

Yes, I most definitely do think a writer can find some margin of success without breaking their pocket books. I also think they can find a great deal of success if they know what they're doing. This sort of goes in conjunction when you ask if there are advantages or disadvantages when going the "pricey" way of marketing. It all comes down to the old principle of why spend money if you don't have to? Why offer someone fifty dollars for a service when you can do it yourself for free or next to no cost? To really streamline this: to spread the word about your book (i.e. create word-of-mouth), you can do this for either free or virtually nothing. In my experience, the only really "costly" way of advertising your book deals with sending out review copies (with shipping costs, that's roughly $5-6 a hit; times that out by, say, even just 20 reviewers and already you're over $100), and buying ad space in magazines (though this method hasn't worked for me; I remember reading somewhere that a person needs to see an ad 7 times before they remember it. Yikes!). I think part of the problem is that writers have been brainwashed into thinking they need these deep, deep pockets in order to successfully market their books. That's ludicrous! Okay, I lied. I can see you needing several thousand dollars if you're looking to selling a million or more copies. But just to simply sell your book? No, that can be done very cheaply. All you need to be willing to do is put the time in to do up some posters, make some phone calls to media outlets (or send press releases), internet advertising, etc. So, I suppose, the only real "cost" is *time* and that's where, I think, a lot of new—even experienced—writers fall short. Any writer would rather spend all their time creating and none of their time marketing, but like I always say, unless you're Grisham or King or Rowling—you're gonna have to get out there and sell your book like there's no tomorrow. It's the only way you'll see success. Even big firms won't sink much money, if any, into marketing you when you're new on the scene. Most writers end up using a significant portion of their advance for marketing expenses. The best way to sell a book is word-of-mouth and there are many, many ways of spreading the word and getting people talking (that, and writing a good book helps, too).

Regarding any scams to be aware of: the only thing I can think of is to be wary of anyone offering to market you in the same way you can market yourself for free (or little cost), but end up charging you your life savings for it. Again, why pay someone to do something for you that you can do for yourself for free? It doesn't make sense. But there are a lot of "services" out there that prey on new writers, make them think they can't market their book without a specific "service" or "package" when, in reality, they're completely unnecessary or, once more, something the author can do on their own. I'd be leery of "marketing your website for you" offers (as you can do this stuff on your own) and marketing "packages" from subsidy POD presses. Those would be my top two.

Hope the above helped.

Sincerely,

Darryl Sloan

July 29, 2006

Dear Darryl:

So sorry for the late reply. This past week I had some Coscom Entertainment deadlines and personal deadlines to attend to. In fact, I completed one of my major tasks today and that is a short story for a speculative fiction Christian anthology that I sold recently. My only concern is that the maximum word count was 5000 words and my first draft is 10,608!! But if it's the Lord's will for this story to appear in the anthology, then there's nothing to fear.

I agree in that youths today, like you said in regards to those attending Clounagh, are a far cry from what they were six years ago. But I side with you in that I'm careful not to "tar all kids with the same brush." It's funny that you mention that because each time I sit down to do a "Human Ailments" segment for *Coscomment*, I always ask myself on some level, "Are people going to think I'm a judgmental idiot for coming across that *all* people behave ill-mannered or have these huge gaping flaws?" Of course

I don't mean those segments as "all of humanity sucks and I'm the golden boy." That's sort of the race we Christians have to run, though, and by that I mean that the second a Christian points out "what's wrong" with society, we're suddenly accused of being "holier than thou." Which is never my intent, of course. The Lord Himself knows I've made a huge mess of things and truly didn't deserve His salvation. Thankfully, He loves(ed) me enough to sacrifice Himself for my sins, take the judgment upon Himself so I wouldn't have to be condemned. Amazing, when you think of it. (I've also been having revelations lately of how big and how deep God's love for us is. Truly mind-boggling when you get right down to it. Or, as an old friend pointed out to me in late May, the odds of God doing what He did are quite slim when you think about it. The context of his statement was purely based on the standpoint/idea of an almighty God taking judgment upon Himself to re-bridge the gap between Him and His creation rather than, say, smiting us all or saying, "You disobeyed now face my wrath," and starting over. Right there, that's love. Huge love. Deep love. Profound love.)

Evil is a real force operating in the human heart, like you said. Now here's a "holier than thou" statement: when one walks closer with God—as most, if not all Christians can relate—the more we see how foul we really are in comparison to His Holiness. Even stuff I thought of as "unsinful" previously has now been called into the light and revealed for what they truly are. I'm disgusted with myself every time. But I'm also thankful that God's giving me these revelations so I can deepen my relationship with Him. It's all a process, man.

The Way of the Fog is now out-of-print, yes. From the start, it was meant to be a limited release whether that was limited copies or for a "limited amount of time." In the novel's case, as it turned out, it was both. (I do, however, have some leftover copies, if you're interested.) However, the timing for my pulling it from print was perfect as for the good part of this year, and part of last, I was seeking to sell it to a mass market publisher as I strongly feel it has mass market potential. On the 20th of July I received notice from a prestigious literary agency in New York that they wanted to see the first fifty pages of it so I mailed them off this past Sunday. I truly and sincerely hope I can gain representation from this firm because it's almost a guaranteed sale to a NY house if I do. But the "sale" is not the driving force. The *Ark of Light* series is meant to draw people closer to God and to, through the course of the story, reveal who Jesus really is and, hopefully, turn souls toward Him. I see a gentleman pretty much weekly for "mentoring" and he said something to me the other day regarding this latest development in the hopeful sale of the book. He said, "When you're doing the Lord's work, you don't have to worry about provision. It'll be there." And that is very true. I mean, I knew that before but when someone says it to you, it becomes more of a reality as it's transcended from the realm of knowledge and into the tangible. So that's what I've been doing: just praying the Lord's Will into this. If He wants it to succeed, I have nothing to worry about. If He doesn't, He'll throw up roadblocks or if He wants another agency to look after it, He'll point me in another direction.

But for those who got the limited edition copy of the book, I'm sure it'll be worth something one day. Just a matter of when.

As always, I enjoy reading your thoughts on *Coscomment.*

In His service,

John Micklefield

August 1, 2006

Dear John:

Thanks for passing along your sermon, "The Second Coming of Jesus Christ." Much obliged. I really appreciated the potency of your opening, detailing Douglas MacArthur's promise to return to the Philippines. Especially what he said when he *did* return: "I have returned." Shudders went up my spine, but in a good way. I had a quick mental flash of Jesus saying those same words when He comes again.

I'm truly glad you preached this, this past Sunday and am sorry I was unable to attend. Would it be possible to let me know of the next time things of an eschatological nature are being preached at Gateway so I can plan to come?

You listed the birth pangs. Very good. (That sounded almost parental, didn't it? Not my intention.) Giving facts and figures like that and displaying for those who are "unaware" just how far along the "birthing wire" we are is a good wake-up call. Most people just think the world has "always been like this," and often say so (especially unbelievers when a believer tries to point out the warning signs of Christ's return). And this is the very sort of comment found in 2 Peter 3:4 that is said to occur in the last days: "*...Where is the promise of his coming? for since the fathers fell asleep, all things continue as they were from the beginning of the creation.*" Truly sad people believe nothing has changed.

What I found intriguing is that the subject of the Second Coming was preached on. What I mean is, it seems that End Times items are all over the news these days in light of the Middle East conflict. End Times-themed media (movies and books) are all the rage even if the "end times" in some of these stories are not

Biblically based but only a shadow of what the Bible says will happen before/during/at End of Days (I'm referring to non-Christian apocalyptic tales). I can't help but wonder if God is sending out one final alert via our favorite entertainment mediums, warning us that the hour is late. It would make sense as He always gives a warning before His wrath is poured out.

Of course I can go on and on here, but given the recent developments in the EU and some of the other facts I sent in my email to Gateway, we're closing in fast. The big one, for me, is the forthcoming ENPI agreement which will span 7 years starting January 2007 running through till 2013. What I find interesting is this reconfirms a ten-nation alliance that was introduced in 1995. What startles me even more is that this agreement is to undergo review in 2010. Further, it is in 2010 that all these worldwide trade agreements we've been hearing about will go into effect. Now I know there's the rule of "no date-setting allowed," but it strikes me that the aforementioned items plus the fact that the EU will soon geographically have the same dominion the Roman Empire did at its peak, that there is currently a Mr. Europe on a mission for peace in the current Middle East crisis, that apostasy is running rampant and immorality is at an all-time high, that people are starting to give thought to the idea of a one-world religion—these things plus all the birth pangs outlined in your sermon *cannot* be coincidence. I'm not a mathematician but it's fair to say the odds of all the prophesied events falling rapidly into place at the same time in history are fairly astronomical if not impossible. What really gets me going is indeed this 2010 business. Seems like a good time to introduce the Mark of the Beast. We have the technology. We just need the enforcement. Perhaps the sudden disappearance of the church might trigger something. Perhaps people will need a way to be tracked so if other disappearances occur, we'll know where they went off to.

If indeed this thing coming up in January 2007 is the start of Daniel's 70th week, we'll soon found out who's right in the Body of Christ regarding the timing of the Rapture. (An item, I noticed, which was left out of your sermon; which is fine as to present a "case of such-and-such timing of the Rapture" is probably 2-3 sermons in itself.)

Anyway, just food for thought on the above. We really should do coffee again so I'm ready when you are.

In His service,

Richard Pulfer

August 8, 2006

Dear Richard:

I hope you can use the following in your article.

For the beginning stages of a marketing plan, you need to ask yourself the simple question of, "Who is my audience and how can I reach them?" Once you determine that, you're good to go. For example, if your book is about an alien invasion, obviously your market—that is main market—are sci-fi geeks. How to locate them is finding out where they meet online (i.e. what message boards or newsgroups; I suggest joining those but not to spam them, but to get in on sci-fi discussions where you can then "plug" your book in your signature line), and where they meet in "real life" (i.e. conventions, bookstores, any sci-fi reading clubs in your area). It's basically about finding out where your audience is and telling them about your book, but also coming off as "one of them" instead of just a salesman. Everyone hates a spammer, online or off-.

For advertising, same thing. At what sci-fi-related outlets can you put up a poster? At what conventions can you hand out a flyer? What magazines do they read? Does your book tie-in and/or is it related to another popular sci-fi property like Stars Wars or something? Can you do a joint promotion with another author who has a larger audience than you?

Keep track of what methods of informing the public work and which ones don't. Use the ones that do, discard the rest. Eventually by doing this, you'll arrive at a winning formula.

Hope the above helps.

In His Service,

Walter Haines

August 11, 2006

Dear Walter:

I was told by my father who in turn was told by Allan Stansall that you were seeking advice on finding a publisher for your manuscript and that Allan would ask my father to get in touch with me to see if I could advise you. Well, with that tongue-twister out of the way, here's my advice: don't publish it!

Kidding.

Seriously, congratulations on finishing your book. Now comes the hard part. The first bit of advice I offer any who ask, "Well, what should I do now?" is to ask yourself what your honest-to-goodness goals are as a writer. Obviously you wish to see your manuscript in book form, but how to start that process is like asking, "What's the best way to find a needle in a haystack?" There is no best way. However, there are good places to "start," hence my question. What are your goals? Is it a) to be rich and famous? b) to publish on the side while working a day job? c) to do nothing once the book is picked up and work on your next one? d) merely just have a finished book to hold and don't care how many copies actually sell? If you can answer the goal question, you have your starting point. But let's assume you're like every other writer out there and dream of hitting the big time. The best starting place is to go and get yourself a literary agent. A good resource for that is the *Guide to Literary Agents* (the most recent one, which is the 2007 edition) put out by Writer's Digest Books. In there you'll find out which agent(s) matches your book the best and how to go about submitting to them. I also strongly urge you to follow their guidelines TO THE LETTER otherwise they'll turn you down flat regardless of how good your book might be.

If you wish to publish on the side while maintaining a day job, then either small press publishing or true self-publishing would be your options. To find a list of small press publishers (and some major ones), try the market listings at www.ralan.com and obey the publishers' guidelines 110%. Should you choose to self-publish, please don't confuse this with vanity and/or subsidy publishing (in short, anytime you pay a "publisher" a fee to "publish" your book). The only self-publishing I suggest is true self-publishing and that is where you, the author, set yourself up as publisher and absorb all editing, layout, cover design, printing, marketing, distribution, etc. costs. And if you go this route, whatever you do, do your research first otherwise you'll sink before you even attempt to swim.

The above is my advice for now, the first being to figure out what your goals are in this business. Once that is established, the path you should take becomes all the more clear.

My door's open for questions if you need it and I hope the above has helped some.

In His service,

Kathy Daley

August 14, 2006

Dear Kathy:

Thank you for pitching the story regarding *Axiom-man* to CBC. They called this morning expressing interest in an interview. When asked if I have a copy of the book, I told them I was planning on sending the files to the printer today (which I did) so should have the proof copy in a couple of weeks. They said to contact them at that time.

So again, thank you.

Sincerely,

Darren Dupras

August 23, 2006

Dear Darren:

Thank you again for agreeing to host an *Axiom-man* book signing at Chapters. Please confirm what time the event will take place. I was thinking 1 or 2pm. Do either of these times work for you? I'm fine with either one.

Thanks in advance.

In His service,

Anneliese Scerri

September 1, 2006

Dear Anneliese:

Thank you for your kind words on *The Way of the Fog.* I'm glad you enjoyed it. Yes, I will be finishing the story though it won't be a trilogy but rather around six to eight books long. At present, I'm aiming for a December 2007 release of Book Two, which at this point is tentatively titled, *The Lights of the North.* It will be in hardback like its predecessor.

In regards to the New York thing, that particular person had decided to pass but solely because they did not feel personally close to the work. Two days ago I pitched them on another project and, hopefully, I'll hear back something positive in the near future.

Hope you're doing well and say hi to the family for me.

In His service,

Richard Pulfer

September 1, 2006

Dear Richard:

Thank you for passing along the most recent issue of *Coffee Break for Writers.* I'm glad I was of some help for your article. (And the door's always open, by the way. Whether I have anything of worth to say or not we'll just have to see.)

I'm also glad you enjoyed the information in *Book Marketing for the Financially-challenged Author*. Though I will admit it's somewhat dated (it was originally published as an eBook early 2004), the basics involved are still current.

I do agree on your assessment on links. There is a point of overkill. Focused links would be a more accurate way to go about the link exchange thing, and what I mean is not just focused by way of genre, but even narrower, perhaps dealing only with those with a similar style to yours. It would take some experimenting if such "narrowness" would really work though. But I don't think people should exchange links with every Tom, Dick and Harry who want to link swap (unless one had a miscellaneous section on their website for random links but even then that's pushing it and from what I've read, search engines are wise to such tactics; they prefer *focused* content, including links).

Regarding your question on film trailers, my personal inclination would be to stay away from copyrighted material (though with fan films and other "comic related" trailers, DC or Marvel hasn't said boo; if you lose one fan, you risk losing them all). For your own sake, and despite how cool John Williams's *Superman* theme is, consider using something in the public domain instead. PD music, as far as I'm aware, is up for grabs, no strings attached. I'm actually going to be looking for some for a trailer for my upcoming book, *Axiom-man*, sometime soon. I need to do some more research into the music front first, though, before I move on any of it. Better be safe than sorry. If you end up using copyrighted material, you will risk bringing a lawsuit down on you if you get caught. A cease and desist notice at the very least. Besides, it's bad taste all around to use someone else's work anyway and can totally wreck your reputation as a professional artist. (And in this business, once your reputation is soiled, so is your career for all eternity.)

I wasn't aware you created web comics. Do you presently have anything available online?

Always good to hear from you.

In His service,

James Newham
Breakfast Television

September 5, 2006

Dear Mr. Newham:

Thank you for your interest in having me on *Breakfast Television* to talk about *Axiom-man*. The morning of September 29th sounds great. Can you please advise me as to the approximate time you would need me down at the station before the program?

Yes, I can definitely get you a copy of the book before then. In fact, I should have a shipment coming in any day now, so once it arrives, I'll bring a copy down to the station. Should I make it out to your attention?

Thank you again and I look forward to your reply.

Sincerely,

Audrey Shaffer
The Writers Chatroom

September 10, 2006

Dear Audrey:

Thank you for your email. I'd be delighted to come back as a guest for The Writer's Chatroom. (I'm also thrilled that your subscriber base has doubled since we last spoke.)

October 4th works for me. On September 29th, I have a new book coming out entitled, *Axiom-man* (see my website for details), a superhero novel. This would be perfect timing to discuss the book plus everything else related to this business.

Please let me know of the precise time of the chat and I'll start making announcements on my end.

Thanks again. I look forward to your reply.

Sincerely,

Audrey Shaffer
The Writers Chatroom

September 13, 2006

Dear Audrey:

Axiom-man is a "regular" book in that it's a prose novel. Regarding the comic side of the property, I have a script written and an artist in the wings. The drawing of the story should begin soon.

For a bio, the one of my website is still relevant. Here it is for your use. I've tweaked it a bit for this chat. Let me know if it's satisfactory.

"A.P. Fuchs finished writing his first book, *A Stranger Dead*, at age 19. It was published in 2003. Since then he has written and completed 9 more books, ranging from fiction to non-fiction to poetry. He has written two collaborative novellas as well.

In 2004 he founded Coscom Entertainment, a publishing firm specializing in superhero and speculative fiction.

On September 29th, Fuchs celebrates the release of his new novel, *Axiom-man*, a superhero novel about battling responsibility with destiny, and the emergence of an evil that has haunted the cosmos since the dawn of Time."

Please don't hesitate to contact me if you need anything further. Thanks again.

Sincerely,

Joe Kroeger

September 16, 2006

Dear Joe:

Thank you for placing your order for *Axiom-man* with Shocklines. I plan on asking Matt for the final total of pre-orders on the 29th (thus allowing right up to the 28th for folks to get their pre-orders in so they can get a free poster; so feel free to tell your friends) and then ship out however many he needs that weekend, in turn ensuring books ship from him to the readers early October.

I did a quick double check into your eBook format question and from the formats that Fictionwise lists under "Multiformat," a .rb file is one of them so you shouldn't have a problem downloading it.

Thank you for your enthusiasm for the project, Joe. I truly hope you enjoy the tale (especially near the end as—insider's tip here—it really gives insight into the setup for book two and "what's really going on").

I plan on beginning work on book two shortly, probably sometime early October with a tentative publication date of spring '07. The working title (though subject to change; please keep confidential as I haven't announced it yet) is *Axiom-man: Doorway to Darkness.*

To keep up on Axiom-man news, I started a blog for him at axiomman.blogspot.com. And if you do the Myspace thing, his Myspace address is www.myspace.com/axiomman

Thanks again.

In His service,

Sara
via Myspace.com email

October 1, 2006

Dear Sara:

Thanks again for your message.

In reply to your questions/comments:

Yes, I do think the world is coming to an end soon. I know at first glance that to say such a thing makes me look like a lunatic or one of those guys who walk around ringing a bell with a sign strapped to their body, stating, "The End is Nigh." It's not like that. It's purely based on what the Bible says regarding the Last Days of human history (of which points were only touched upon at *Coscomment* in the entry, "Jesus is Coming Soon"; there are many other proofs occurring as I type this) and what the world will be like just prior to the Second Coming of Jesus Christ. You asked why I would think such a terrible thing? It's not a terrible thing at all. The world ending is not a bad thing in the least provided one is on the side of the Lord (a person is either for Him or against Him; see Luke 11:23). A person does not fear his/her best friend. To say His return is a bad thing is also like saying the promise of peace is a bad thing (which will *only* happen at Christ's coming) or being in the physical presence of God Almighty is a bad thing. Those things certainly cannot be bad. As outlined in my entry, one of the main reasons why Christians get so excited about the end of the world is because our King and best Friend will *finally* be here. Who wouldn't be excited to see their best friend? Another has to do with us being tired of living in a world overrun by sin. I'm not claiming Christians are perfect, by the way, but most people, Christians or not, are sick of all the moral corruption going on, especially these days. The excitement for the final chapter of human history has nothing to do with wishing doom and gloom on the world (though, of course, I can't see the Apocalypse as it's happening being a picnic). It's about what it promises to bring, and that is the Return of the King.

Regarding people not experiencing the life—when this all comes about—that people generations before have had, again, I have to ask what is better: life as it was/is, with hardships and trials intermixed with good times, or rather a life where the Lord Himself is with us all the time in the flesh? I have to go with the latter, personally.

To be clear, my life doesn't revolve around the end of the world. It's just a keen interest of mine. Actually, to look forward to Christ's return is gain for me as the Bible says those who long for His appearing receive a crown (2 Timothy 4:8). I'm also aware that folks have come along in the past stating the End was at hand and now they're dead. As mentioned in my entry, what's significant about all the warning signs the Bible says will happen at the end of Time is that they're all happening simultaneously right now in the year 2006. There is not a single point in history where this has ever happened before. I very well could be wrong and that's fine. But what if I'm right? It's all taken from the Bible and I won't ever say the Bible is wrong. Example, keep your eyes on the European Union. I promise you you'll see some significant things happening from their side of the world very soon, things which have been prophesied to happen thousands of years ago.

You said that those in the past have been wrong, and you're right, but your comment also mirrors what was prophesied to be said in the last days (2 Peter 3:2-4).

I'll have to disagree with the statement about good people—"good" being the operative word—being allowed into the afterlife (Heaven, in the context you stated it). The first reason is that there is not a single good person on this planet, myself included. Why? The Bible says there is no one righteous, no not one (Romans 3:9-11). As well, our "good" works, in God's sight, are nothing but filthy rags (Isaiah 64:6). And we can't get into Heaven by works or good deeds either. Only by grace (Ephesians 2:7-9). These aren't my words. They're God's. God's standard is perfection but we've all missed the mark (Romans 3:23). We've all sinned, whether just once or a million times over, whether we've told a little white lie or have killed somone intentionally. Regardless of what "degree" of sin, it all has the same penalty: death (Romans 6:23). And that means hell. That's what we all deserve. Thankfully, the Lord provided a pardon. This illustration, though a common one, shows what He's done. Let's say you get busted for a drug deal and you're standing in court before the judge. He tells you that you've been found guilty and that you're doomed to jail for the rest of your life or you can go free on bail for $500,000. You're broke so you plead with the judge and tell him you've never done anything else wrong in your entire life and you promise never to cooperate in another drug deal again. Do you think he'll let you slide? No. He'll say to you, "That's good that you won't ever deal drugs again and flood the streets with them, but you still committed the crime and the law needs to be satisfied." You plead with him, begging him for another chance because you don't have $500,000 to put up for bail and you don't know anyone who can help you out. You're screwed. "Too bad," the judge tells you. And just as he's about to slam the gavel down and sentence you to rot in jail, someone you don't know rushes in and plops a huge briefcase on the judge's pulpit. The judge opens it up and the briefcase contains $500,000. You now have a choice. You can either accept the kindness this person has done for you or you can say, "Thanks but no thanks," and let the judge send you off to the pen. Unless someone is crazy, the money would be taken in a heartbeat. Once it's been accepted—the fine paid—the law's been satisfied and justice has been served and the judge is *obligated* to set you free. This is the same thing Jesus did a little under 2000 years ago for you and me. He satsified God's law by paying the penalty of sin for us (death) so you and I and everyone else wouldn't have to. Now each of us has a choice. Do we accept that He paid the price or do we say,

"Thanks but no thanks," and go to jail (hell)? If we choose to accept what He's done, all we need to do is a) admit our need (that we've sinned against Him), b) repent (say sorry and mean it by turning from our sins), c) believe that Jesus paid the price for us at the cross and proved the payment was enough by rising from the grave three days later, d) pray to Him and ask Him to forgive you and come into your life through the Holy Spirit (receive Him as Lord and Savior). It's the only way we'll escape what we truly deserve.

As much as God is a God of love and mercy (He provided a pardon for us through His Son after all), He's also a good God and one of justice. He wouldn't be a good God if He didn't call people into account for what they've done. Many will hope that either upon death or at the end of the world that His love and mercy will be what saves them. In the end, it'll be what condemns them because they didn't accept His pardon while there was still time. His very goodness will see that the law is satisfied.

Please note all of the above is intended warmly.

I'm not quite sure what you meant when you said God brings blind men into the world but punishes them with they trip and fall. Was this meant to be allegory or literal? The context doesn't reveal it.

I noticed in your message you spelled God "G-d." Are you Jewish? If so, I choose to bless you in the Name of the Lord. (And if not, I choose to bless you anyway.)

I hope you had a good weekend.

Best,

Richard Pulfer

October 5, 2006

Dear Richard:

I, too, have thought of using Youtube.com as part of my marketing campaign, especially for my forthcoming trailer for the Axiom-man novel.

As per your question, yes, the "financially-challenged" writer could use Youtube to put up trailers for his/her own work provided they owned *every* last frame of the video in question. To put up any other video or audio or picture where you were not the creator without express permission from the original creator of the video/audio/picture, puts you in the position of copyright infringement. I'm not sure 100% what would be considered "free use," and thus I personally wouldn't risk it. I'd just use whatever is utterly and completely yours and yours alone.

Hope this helps.

Good to hear from you.

Sincerely,

Elisha Cumbers
The Herald

October 5, 2006

Dear Elisha:

Thank you again for stopping by today to interview me for *The Herald.* I had a great time and was quite pleased with the questions asked. (I hope you were equally pleased with the answers given; they were the truth.)

I admit I'm not 100% sure regarding the pictures taken so, just in case, please find enclosed with this message a couple of shots of Axiom-man to use as you please for the article. However, if you feel the pictures we took are fine as is, then by all means use those. I just wanted to provide you with a couple of alternatives should the pictures not pan out.

Please let me know if you need anything further or have any questions.

Thanks again.

Sincerely,

Glenn Walker
Comic Widows

October 6, 2006

Dear Glenn:

Thank you for coming by the Writer's Chatroom two nights ago. It's always great when people show up and, in the case of the *Axiom-man* release, when comic fans show up. (Thank you again for pre-ordering your copy, by the way. You'll also be receiving a free poster with your order.)

Today I'll be mailing off your door prize: *Magic Man.* It's a tale I think you'll enjoy in that while it's not "comic booky" by any means, it does have a comic book feel, as comic book-type worlds have a large influence upon my writing. *Magic Man* was a chapbook I released back in January of 2005 and was received well by readers. I don't say that to brag but rather to inform you that since the character did go over very well, I decided to pit Axiom-man up against him in the forthcoming comic book one-shot entitled, *Axiom-man: Of Magic and Men.* This won't be available until sometime in 2007, however. But, at least this way you'll be able to familiarize yourself with the Magic Man and will know his back story, which isn't revealed in the one-shot. The Magic Man will also be making an appearance in a story called "Below" for the upcoming *Raw Meat* anthology put out by Wicked Karnival. Publication date was supposed to be this year but it looks more like early next year as, last I heard, the signature sheet for the book was still making its rounds to the authors.

It wasn't until your email did I realize you were the one who ran *Comic Widows.* Though at present I don't have any superhero comic book(s) (or any non-superhero comic book(s), for that matter) "out there," I do have the *Axiom-man* prose novel. Feel free to review it for your site, if you'd like. As well, I offer myself as an interview subject should the mood suit you in the future.

Thank you again for coming by the chat and I hope you enjoy both the books coming your way.

In His service,

Hatch Tarr
LOP Magazine

October 8, 2006

Dear Hatch:

Thank you for your interest in *Axiom-man* (and in myself as well). I'd be more than happy to take part in an interview and likewise allow LOP to review my work. Please contact me at coscomentertainment@gmail.com and I'll send a PDF of *Axiom-man* to you.

Thank you again for getting in touch with me. I look forward to your reply.

Sincerely,

Hatch Tarr
LOP Magazine

October 13, 2006

Dear Hatch:

Thanks for your continued interested in *Axiom-man.* Please find attached the eBook edition of the novel. Please note (and this merely a formal disclaimer) the eBook is for review purposes and your eyes only.

Looking forward to hearing your thoughts on it.

Sincerely,

David Bradley

October 19, 2006

Dear David:

I'm very glad to hear you're finding *Book Marketing for the Financially-challenged Author* useful. When I had sent out *A Stranger Dead* postcards as part of my freebie offer, the back had the book's synopsis and ordering info (title, author name, ISBN). One side had the info, the other had a lot of white space so I could make out a personal note to whomever.

To be honest, I'm not sure if I have any left. Rather, I'm not sure where they are. At present, *A Stranger Dead* is out-of-print so I don't need to plug the title anymore. If I stumble across an extra postcard in the office, I'll let you know and send you one.

As a suggestion for what to include on the back, no matter what, is the aforementioned ordering info to make your title easier for bookstores to get in (if they don't have it already), plot synopsis and some room so you could write a note to whomever you send it to.

The name of the game is making folks aware of your book and postcards are a great way to do that. You can also mail a bunch of them to various bookstores with a typed note (which you can paste onto the card) asking if they'd be willing to order in copies of your novel. It would also be good to include any endorsements, if you have any, to help add credibility to your book. Bookstores, more often than not, are reluctant to order in a title if they don't know who you are.

Sincerely,

Jeff Davis

October 23, 2006

Dear Jeff:

Thanks for writing. Sales for *Axiom-man* are going quite well. Thanks for asking.

I had a plan to release a second book on marketing but with all the other stuff I have on the go, I haven't had the chance to complete it so, sorry, I don't really have an answer as to when it will come out. However, I do have a copy of *Book Marketing for the Financially-challenged Author*, if you're interested.

Congratulations on your decision to take the plunge into self-publishing. You had asked for advice. Honestly, it's a huge topic.

My first bit of advice would be research all you can about the publishing field and what's expected of publishers once they have a title out there. You need to know what you're getting yourself into. I wouldn't want you diving in then all of a sudden finding yourself drowning and/or spending a fortune with little or no return. That, and be sure you know what's required of you in regards to running your own publishing business (business registrations, ISBNs, LCCNs (or CIPs in Canada), copyright info, etc.). My second bit of advice is to find out all you can about book production and what it takes to put out a quality product, namely the editing of the manuscript, interior layout, cover design and layout. As well, learn what you can about book printing and find something that works within your budget. The *big* thing, of course, is then planning out how you'll market the title. There's no sense having a basement full of books and no readers. Set yourself realistic goals in this regard and be honest with yourself as to how many you think you can sell. If you can't move at least 500 copies, it might not be worth it, depending on how your profit margins work out. I strongly suggest having a solid marketing plan before you put the book into production.

The above is for starters but it's also a step most author/publishers don't take, which then gives way to them forking over a lot of money and never seeing any return on the time they put in to create their product (and, yes, it's a "product" now and not a book).

In His service,

Joe Kroeger

October 28, 2006

Dear Joe:

Nanci Kalanta over at *Horrorworld* just emailed me a copy of your review of *Axiom-man*. Thank you very much for the positive review. I'm thrilled that you enjoyed the novel to such an extent. I wasn't aware *Horrorworld* reviewed superhero material. Either way, I'm glad folks will be able to see what you thought of it.

I'm not sure what your review arrangement with *Horrorworld* are or what rights to the review they hold, but if you're able to do with the review as you please, I was hoping to be able to use a blurb from your review for *Axiom-man*'s Amazon.com page and future Axiom-man publications. Is this possible? I'll also inquiry Nanci on this subject.

As per your statement in the review stating you hope to see more of Axiom-man in the future, you'll be pleased to know that you will. If all goes to plan, 2007 will see the publication of the Axiom-man vs Magic Man one-shot comic book entitled, "Of Magic and Men." It will also see the publication of *Axiom-man II: Doorway to Darkness* (of which roughly 10,000 words are complete). More is to come and I'm glad to have you on board as one of my readers.

Take care.

In His service,

Susie Moloney

November 8, 2006

Dear Susie:

Thank you for stopping by my table at Coles this past weekend. It was a pleasure meeting you.

The other day I checked out your website and snooped around. Then I went to see your bibliography and discovered you are the author of *A Dry Spell.* Turns out I had your book already on my to-be-read pile so I've moved it up in the pecking order and will be reading it shortly.

I was also wondering if sometime in the future you'd be open to meeting for coffee and "talking shop"? You can tell me all about New York and I can fill you in on the exciting life of a small-presser. Kind of a "worlds collide" conversation when you think of it. Said with a smile, of course.

Anyway, once again it was great talking to you and I hope your week's going great so far and you're plugging away at your keyboard.

In His service,

Glenn Walker
Comic Widows

November 8, 2006

Dear Glenn:

Glad to hear *Axiom-man* and *Magic Man* arrived safe and sound. You can never tell with the post office these days and just recently I had part of an order get damaged (and partially lost) on me due to post office inadequacies. Again, glad to know they came (though I am sorry you had to wait to get to them because of your neighbor's vacation; always someone else getting out of town and never ourselves, eh?).

I'd be delighted to take you up on you taking me up on that interview offer. Whenever you're ready is fine with me. I also look forward to what you have to say if/when *Axiom-man* is reviewed for *Comic Widows*.

Take care.

In His service,

Brian Michael Bendis

November 16, 2006

Dear Brian:

How are you?

I'm writing you for two reasons, the first being more "fanboy" oriented, the second being business.

Okay, the first:

I'm really enjoying your *Ultimate Spider-man* run (read the first three volumes so far) and what I've found particularly interesting/noticed is that, being a novelist myself, you seem to have taken an intentional (or perhaps unintentional, depending on how you write your scripts) "novel" approach to writing the series. What I picked up on, aside from the story itself, was a) the whole thing is basically one big story just broken up into 22 or so page segments (I'm referring to all three volumes), b) your character development. What I mean on the latter is your introduction of characters earlier on (i.e. Otto Octavius) but then not giving that character major screen time or a story arc until much later. Same thing happens in novels: introducing the secondary characters briefly first then giving that character a bigger part later once some time has been spent with the protagonist. I must say I enjoy your approach (the "novel scope" of it) better than the "Well, it's a new month so what bad guy can we bring in or what brand new story without reference to previous tales can we do?" Granted, *Ultimate Spider-man* is a re-launch of sorts so you do have the advantage compared to "regular" monthlies. Anyway, good job. I also have your book, *Torso*, on my shelf and it's one of my favorites of "non-superhero" graphic novels.

The second reason I'm writing you is to see if you'd be interested in blurbing my superhero novel, *Axiom-man*? An independent release, the novel was launched September 2006 and has been well-received by readers. (For Axiom-man news and "what's happened so far," please visit axiomman.blogspot.com.) Secondly, here is the URL to a surprise review done by Horror World (which caught me off guard as they review primarily horror/dark fantasy publications and not superhero work). The link is http://horrorworld.org/reviews.htm (scroll about halfway down for the review).

I'd also like to mention previous work of mine has received endorsements from the likes of legendary fantasy scribe Piers Anthony and *New York Times* bestselling author Douglas Clegg, along with other notables in the literary field. I only mention this as a point of credentials, nothing more.

The plot synopsis for *Axiom-man* is as follows:

One night Gabriel Garrison was visited by a nameless messenger who bestowed upon him great power, a power intended for good. Once discovering what this power was and what it enabled him to do, Gabriel became Axiom-man, a symbol of hope in a city that had none.

One night after a routine patrol, a mysterious black cloud appears over the city. Flying over to investigate it, Axiom-man is stopped short when the cloud's presence shakes him to the core. An electrifying fear emanates from the cloud and he can barely get near it. Quickly, the cloud takes flight and leads him on a wild goose chase throughout the city, only to flee from him in the end. Almost immediately after the cloud's appearance, a new hero arises, Redsaw, clad in a black cape and cowl. The people, now enamored with this new super-powered marvel, seem to have forgotten about Axiom-man and all he's done for them.

Except something's wrong. That same fear that emanated from the cloud drips off Redsaw like a foul smell and Axiom-man can barely get close to him without feeling ill.

What is Redsaw's agenda and who is he? And why is it every time Axiom-man gets close to him it feels as if his powers are being sucked away?

As if that wasn't enough, Gabriel's day job hasn't gotten any easier. His co-worker and the woman he adores, Valerie

Vaughan, has little interest in him, and his boss has made it clear that one more day late to work will be the day he cleans out his desk. Then there's the new trainee, Gene Nemek. What is his fascination with Redsaw and why is he never around when Redsaw appears?

From flying over city streets and soaring at dizzying heights, to balancing a secret identity with destiny, Axiom-man must discover what Redsaw's presence means and how it ties into the messenger's life-altering visit before the city—and the world—are enamored with an evil that has haunted the cosmos since the dawn of Time.

Should you be interested in reviewing my book, please also be aware I have a standing policy in regards to those who agree to take a look at my material, and that is should you agree, you are by no means under any obligation to offer an endorsement should you not enjoy the work for any reason. I'm well aware this is a business where you can't please everybody and as far as I know, you might be one of those people. I just kindly request that should you feel you cannot offer a blurb of some kind to please let me know so I'm not left wondering. As well, of course, there would be no hard feelings and I'd still read *Ultimate Spider-man.*

What I'm primarily seeking in terms of a blurb would be an endorsement for the character himself which I could use to help promote the current release and also forthcoming sequels (the first of which is about a quarter done as of this writing). But, of course, I'd be thankful for whatever you decide to offer.

Thank you in advance for your time and consideration. I look forward to your reply.

Sincerely,

Jeff Davis

November 28, 2006

Dear Jeff:

I'm truly glad to hear you're loving *Axiom-man.* To be honest, it was a novel I wasn't quite sure that would be received all too well. Perhaps because it was so intensely personal to me (I've had the idea in my head for thirteen years), I was afraid that if folks didn't like it, they actually wouldn't like *me*, seeing as how Gabriel Garrison is very much like me in a lot of ways, likewise Axiom-man is very much the ideal I hope to become. A trend I've noticed in my work is that the stories that I'm hesitant on (for whatever reason) tend to be the ones people love, and the ones I'm sure of tend to be the ones people either like or are just perceived as "okay" and "so-so." Weird, but that's how it is, it seems.

I'm sorry to hear Borders gave you such a hard time in getting the book in and you eventually had to go to Barnes and Noble. Frankly, though, that doesn't surprise me given the "elitist" attitude that plagues the publishing industry, ranging from writers to agents and publishers and also from the bookstores. Small pressers like myself have a hard time competing with an industry that makes it almost impossible for the little guy to make any headway, namely due to finances. I'm sure the problem Borders had was the book was non-returnable and the discount wasn't as steep as they would have liked (so they could make more money than the people who actually *make* the book). I'm even sorrier to hear they wouldn't offer you the basic customer service (and decency) to get the title in for you, who is the customer.

To answer your question, I chose to make Gabriel a credit card representative because it was a position I myself once held and one I really enjoyed. It's also a job—telephone customer service—that I know very well as the majority of my career when I held a day job was based in a call centre environment. It's great to hear your friends at work want to read it. By all means, pass the book around or, better, encourage them to order a copy through Barnes and Noble or via their website (or Amazon or Shocklines). Or if they do read your copy and like it, encourage them to get one for their own shelf as a support to the author. Regardless, I'm thankful people are reading the book and that I'm able to share the character with any who are interested.

The novel's interior was designed in MSWord. It's a bit tricky to use for book design but I've established an effective system that works for me and, when you compare my books to ones designed by Indesign (which most publishers use), they're comparable. I have yet to see a difference between the two programs that would make me want to run out and get Indesign for myself. The cover was designed in Photoshop and the colorist, who does freelance for Marvel, colored it in Photoshop as well.

I look forward to your thoughts on *Axiom-man* once you read the novel in its entirety.

Thanks for writing.

In His service,

Wayne Guindon

December 8, 2006

Dear Wayne:

I agree. Most people have at least one good book in them. The real trick when it comes to any form of creative output—and, as like you said—is the actual *doing* of it. Too many people, as has been my experience, talk and talk about creating this and creating that but most of the time that creation just stays as a lump of ideas in their head and never takes on any real and tangible form. And in today's easy-to-use media-structured society, there's no excuse for not getting anything done. To a large degree, turning an idea into reality doesn't cost all that much.

I've come across too many people who say they don't have time due to a) their day job, b) family, c) time with friends, d) etc., to actually do what they've been wanting to do all their lives. And these then end up becoming the people that no one likes talking to anyway because at some point during the conversation you find out how dissatisfied they are with life and if only they could have "followed their dream" would things have been better. I'm a realist and know that most people aren't doing what they want to do for a living. I also *realize* that it's their fault that it is that way, too. To me, if you have a goal or dream and know clearly what that goal or dream is, the onus is on you to go after it *without* excuse. Dreams are never handed over to people and if they are, it's always by fluke and by getting-struck-by-lightning odds. If other things are getting in someone's way to actually pursue their goals, well, then I guess that goal or dream wasn't as important to them as they thought, right?

If something truly matters to someone, they'll go no holds barred to get it.

I say this from experience. You have to "go and get it" without excuse. See it through or it'll pass you by.

Do it.

In His service,

David Brollier

December 8, 2006

Dear David:

Thanks for writing and I'm very happy you, as you say, loved *Axiom-man*. I also found your comment about wanting to know *why* Axiom-man got his powers interesting as that's exactly what's explained in book two. When I first began the series, my goal for the first book was to explain "how" Axiom-man got his powers in those flashback sequences. The second book was meant to explain "why," utilizing the same flashback method. The same applies to Redsaw. The first book really is a touch on the surface when it comes to the overall cosmic story that is the Axiom-man saga. The second book really delves deep into that now that I have the origin stuff out of the way. This freedom also allows me to really get things going as now the characters are already established powers-wise and I don't have to spend time explaining how they got that way.

In regards to the Axiom-man story being a, as you put it, "beautifully crafted analogy of spiritual warfare," the truth is, that was unintentional. Like fellow author Jon Klement once told me (and he might have been quoting someone else), "All the good stories are reflections of the Great Story." The truth is, everything that folks have enjoyed story-wise always reflect the Biblical account of the Savior in some way. Just look at Superman. For the Axiom-man universe, I don't plan on making it a "Bible-thumping" Christian series by any means. Will Christianity or an echo of it play a blatant part in it? Perhaps. I have some ideas but I'm trying to keep my witness in this series low key. It has nothing to do with being ashamed, but as most Christians will say, the best witness in fiction is the subtle witness. Unbelievers nine times out of ten will hate a book that's nothing but a super long Bible tract. Like the Word says, to those who are perishing the Gospel is a foul stench. But to those who are saved, it's utterly pleasant. Or something like that. My mind and heart have always been fond of the battle between good and evil. That's why I was attracted to superheroes back when I was a kid. Any resemblance Axiom-man's story has to spiritual warfare is coincidental, though the series does take place in the real world where such spiritual powers of good and evil truly exist.

I have no trouble at all with you creating a superhero of your own and from the description you gave me, it's obviously a Bible-based superhero. Which is fine, believe me. My only word of caution is not to make it stupid or campy. From what I've seen, those who don't believe in Jesus view that sort of stuff—Christian fiction or Christian-based characters (ie. Bible-man)—as hokey and dumb, and to be honest, they usually have a good reason as it seems a lot of that stuff revolves around the "a happy-go-lucky God." What I mean is, when I see such characters in Christian bookstores, I always get the mental image of a bunch of children holding hands, spinning in a circle around a rainbow, singing, "La la la la la la, we love God and He loves us. La la la la la." Though, of course, that statement is true, it does ring of camp. I think the challenge to any Christian working on Bible-based fiction is to make Christianity cool again. Too many people conjure up the idea that the Bible is boring or is about standing behind a pew singing hymns when, really, it's not about that at all and if you look at the amazing supernatural stuff that occurred during the few couple centuries of the church, it's really quite amazing what went down. A lot of it reads like a fantasy novel (not that it is fantasy, by any means, but the supernatural elements are there). Have you read the account of Polycarp's martyrdom? Amazing what happened. I won't spoil it for you but it definitely put the authorities of the day at a loss. So though the "God is love" is part of it, there's so much more to it that most people overlook. And that's sad because, whether people like it or not, Christianity is what our reality is based on. The Biblical record is true. All of it.

So, yeah, if you do a blatant Bible superhero, go for it. Just make him cool.

In His service,

Steven Jorgenson

December 12, 2006

Dear Steven:

Heard about you losing your copy of *Axiom-man* on Shocklines. I'm glad you recovered it and, according to the old "what're you reading now" thread, are finished it. Once more, I hope you liked it.

Yes, unfortunately in book one there are no images of Redsaw. Sometime in the future I may do a limited special "boxed" edition of book one and it would include some artwork and other sketchbook material, but until then, readers won't be seeing an image of Redsaw till the cover of book two (tentatively scheduled for a June/July release in 2007).

However, I do have a sketch of him, which is attached to this message. Please keep the file confidential. You'll also need to use your imagination as the sketch is only in pencil and the parts that are to be inked black are marked with a X. The portions not marked with a X are blood red.

Redsaw does wear a half-mask. Axiom-man does not. As per the cover, Axiom-man's mask is full-face but with the top cut off so his hair can hang out. Fortunately, given the nature of his powers, his hair serves as part of his disguise because, while Axiom-man, his hair takes on a blue-ish hue whereas while Gabriel Garrison, it's just plain brown. (And it's combed differently; parted down the middle for Axiom-man, parted on the side for Gabriel.)

Thanks for checking *Axiom-man* out.

In His service,

Steve Doyle

December 22, 2006

Dear Steve:

Thank you for the kind words for *Book Marketing for the Financially-challenged Author.* I'm glad you found the information useful, as that was my purpose in writing it: to help other authors find ways to market their books without busting their wallets. I'm sure you'll put the information to good use.

I'd also be more than happy to swap links with you. I'll notify my webmaster to add yours when the next update is done.

Feel free to link to one or all of the following websites:

www.apfuchs.com
www.coscomentertainment.com
axiomman.blogspot.com
coscomentertainment.blogspot.com
www.myspace.com/apfuchs
www.myspace.com/axiomman

Thanks again and have a very blessed Christmas.

In His service,

Lee Pederson
Onzo Media

December 23, 2006

Dear Lee:

Thank you for thinking of me to send a promotional copy of *How to Be a Nonconformist* to. It arrived last night. I haven't had a chance to read it yet but did flip through it. I also appreciate your compliments regarding the similarities between our companies. I hope whatever you've learned from Coscom Entertainment will serve you and your company well in the future.

I also found it amusing that you *did* think of me in regards to *How to Be a Nonconformist.* Being a "nonconformist" is what we self-publishers have been accused of being many times in the past. The common argument is that those of us who do self-publish believe we have something so precious literary-wise that we don't dare take it to a traditional firm and run the risk of them meddling with it. I do tend to agree with that argument insofar as that there are a few authors who feel that way about their work, typically those authors who write what I've labeled as "nonsensical fiction," the type of stories (or poetry) that are just plain weird for weird sake and little else. In my case, I chose the self-publishing route partly out of naivety at the time I got into the publishing side of this business (2003) and partly because I didn't want to go through the submitting, waiting, submitting, waiting, etc. process and not see a book of mine in print for possibly years on end. I figured I'd begin to build an audience straight away and then proceed to New York. It has worked, though, as doors in the New York community have been opened to me as a result of my self-publishing efforts. I could also be, however, a rare exception in that regard.

Back to "nonsensical fiction." I live in Winnipeg and our art community is extremely strong and well-supported by locals. Though such support has served me well (especially when it came to the release of my local-based superhero, Axiom-man), I also see it as a bit of a risk on the city's part in that, though support of the art scene is important (for any city), it also encourages "artists" to proceed with work that truly is nonsensical. This would cover any medium and not necessarily book-type work. I've encountered many "artists" in the past, namely at open-mic poetry nights and film screenings and they're all cut from the same cloth. All the guys are carbon copies of each other: Buddy Holly glasses, plaid shirts and ill-fitting jeans. The girls are the same: spiky hair with strange-colored streaks, wearing dresses from the '70s or '80s. Why? To me that makes absolutely no sense. If only one "artistic" guy or girl dressed that way out of all the "artistic" guys and girls, then okay, fine. That's their style. But since it seems to be an epidemic to all "set themselves apart from the norm" types, it rings of pretension and a misunderstanding of what being an artist is all about. The truth of the matter is, an artist—a *true* artist, regardless of the medium you work in—is one who is a) honest about *themselves* and b) is honest in the *presentation* of their work and doesn't try to make it weird or "set it apart" solely for arts sake.

Anyway, I'm off point a little here, but as for us self-publishers being labeled as "nonconformists" (though never called such to our faces but it's been certainly implied), I know that in the case of myself, any nonconformity on my part has been purely unintentional. The fact of the matter is, when one is responsible for putting out one's own work, 9.9 times out of 10 that person doesn't have the same resources and financial abilities that, say, traditional New York publishing has. So we improvise and in so doing perhaps pave a few inroads and discover means of publishing and promotion that your typical New York-based publishing firm doesn't employ. It's not a slight against them by any means but since New York-based publishing is the standard this industry is based upon, they are used as the benchmark in this business and anything that goes outside said standard is suddenly labeled as "wrong" or "evil."

(As a side note, what I do suspect is happening when us "nonconformists" are publicly slammed—usually by those who are "conformists" or "are conforming"—is that they see us making do just fine with what we have and, in some cases, achieving the same level of success "nonconforming" as they had "conforming" to a system that, in my opinion, doesn't work as well as it could, perhaps even should, and so are jealous to some degree, whether they are aware of that jealousy or not.)

Thank you again for the book and I'll give it a read as soon as I complete the other two books I'm engrossed in at the moment.

I wish you a Merry Christmas and all the best in the coming New Year.

Sincerely,

Ps. You also mentioned the above book was for my review. Were you hoping for a write-up of some sort from me? Please let me know. Thanks again.

F. Scott

December 29, 2006

Dear F. Scott:

Thanks for the cudos. Did you read *Axiom-man* or were you commenting on the plot synopsis? (Just curious.) If you did read it, I thank you kindly.

I think I posted on the Crows message board once or twice in the past but never really got into it. Though I like music, it's not really "my thing" in that I always have to a song blaring on the speakers. I used to write to music but now just enjoy a quiet room without any outside influences.

Counting Crows heavily influenced my love story, April, in terms of tone as the novel is all about meeting someone and really and truly and deeply connecting with them whether it works out in the end or not.

Hope you had a great Christmas and all the best in '07.

Sincerely,

Nick Cato

January 6, 2007

Dear Nick:

Thanks for your note about *Axiom-man*. I'm very glad that you enjoyed it, particularly your comment about it being a LOAD (emphasis yours) of fun. That seems to be the consensus regarding this book, and that's fine with me. It was my first novel after doing *The Way of the Fog*, the first in that epic fantasy series of mine. *The Way of the Fog* was a huge novel, about 236,000 words, loaded with history and culture and detail upon detail. With *Axiom-man*, I wanted to do something light and fun, something someone could read without thinking all too much and breeze through relatively quickly. You'll be pleased to know that as of this writing, the sequel is approximately 3/4 complete and is currently scheduled for a June/July 2007 release. As I've mentioned to a few others, now that the origin stuff is out of the way, I can go no-holds barred into the "comic booky" kind of stuff action and stake-wise in this second outting. As well, with this second novel, character growth occurs big time for all three principal characters (Gabriel, Valerie and Oscar). That's all I'll say about that. Also, coming later this year is *Axiom-man Episode #0: First Night Out*, which explores his, well, first night out as hinted at in the origin novel. Now I get to show the reader what happened the first time he dawned the tights. It'll be a chapbook, probably 6,000-7,000 words and I plan on publishing it alongside *Axiom-man II: Doorway to Darkness.*

Thanks for the tip about doing a comic shop tour. Now that my book signings are all done for the title (I logged in 7 in 2006, with perhaps one final one later this month or next), I can focus on the comic shops. I know I'll definitely be hitting them up when the Axiom-man one-shot comic book comes out. It's called *Of Magic and Men* and it features Axiom-man facing off against the Magic Man (the lead villain of a chapbook of the same name which was released January 2005).

Any Christian symbolism that was in *Axiom-man*, to be honest, was purely unintentional. The only "intentional" Christianity I threw in there was when the messenger tells Gabriel that he serves the One True God. My goal, of course, is make the Axiom-man tales as realistic as possible and that includes staging these stories in a reality as close to the one that you and I live in. And since God and Christ and the Holy Spirit are a part of our reality, so They will be a part of Axiom-man's reality, too.

Again, glad you enjoyed it. Thanks.

In Christ,

Cynthia MacKinnon
The Writers Caf Press

January 10, 2007

Dear Cynthia:

Here are the answers to your interview questions, separated by number. I hope the following is what you were looking for. Thanks for this interview opportunity.

1. As cliché a response as this is, the reason I'm a writer is because I *have to.*
I've "lived in my head" ever since I could remember, coming up with one fantasy after another. It was always about stories to me and when I was old enough to realize one could making a living "making stuff up," I started to pursue that route. My first intention was to be a comic book artist. I even went to school for it but when that school didn't fulfill their end of the bargain by not teaching us all they had promised (and charged us a life savings for it to boot), I switched my attention to the written word, at the time bitter toward anything "artistic." That was back in early-to-mid 2000 and I've been writing seriously since. I began publishing in 2003.

2. Biblical speculative fiction is a new venue for me and I'm relatively new at it with three Christian pieces to my name in that genre. My first was the first novel my *Ark of Light* series entitled *The Way of the Fog.* That was published in June 2005, with the second novel due out December 2007. Since then I've done only two Bic-spec-fic novelettes, one called *The Last Gentile*, which is unpublished, the other being *Undeniable*, which will appear in the *Light at the Edge of Darkness* anthology sometime in 2007.

My goal with writing Biblical speculative fiction is, the Lord willing, to make Jesus "cool" again, and by that I mean to show others that Jesus isn't just some Guy who acts and lives at a distance from us and is the focal point of "religion," but rather is the One who can be up close and personal if we let Him, and we can have a personal relationship with Someone who is God, who has an incredibly interesting history, and has a depth to Him that no other figure in history (both past, present and future) has.

3. The real issue, to me, is not so much the label of "speculative fiction," but rather what's contained within that fiction. On the surface, most Christians think that if a book or short story doesn't have a "Christian" label, it's suddenly off limits. But these are also the same people who enjoy *Star Wars* and *Lord of the Rings*, both of which are clearly stories that don't talk about Jesus or the Bible or whatnot.

I think that Christian fiction and speculative fiction are very compatible in that speculative fiction provides an "other worldly" venue to express one's Christian views. There's no shame in doing a sci-fi novel which features a Christian crew on a starship and aliens (even though aliens—intelligent ones, anyway, for who knows what types of creatures lurk on other worlds?—aren't "Biblically correct"). The issue is the message. What are you promoting? If you're doing fantasy and are promoting magic, then you've got a problem as the Bible states that magic is off limits and who are you to lead others astray. However, if you're doing fantasy and using allegory (i.e. *Chronicles of Narnia*) then you're all right. Same with horror and the supernatural. Are you glorifying evil or are you portraying supernatural evil as it really is but also showing the flipside, and that is Christ's power over it?

I think the problem—and this is a blanket statement—most Christians have with speculative fiction is that they really don't know what the story is about but since it's secular (or secularly labeled), they automatically give it a bad rap. We live in a society where believers and unbelievers alike base their opinions and thoughts on a particular form of entertainment solely on what others say is good or bad. I like to challenge individuals to make decisions for themselves. Does a story interest you? Then check it out. In a believer's case, if the book jacket contains something that you know Jesus Himself wouldn't look at then set it back down.

It's a fine line because the Bible also says that we as believers should not do anything that might cause another brother to stumble. This can also be extended to unbelievers who are watching our every move (which is what happens when you confess Christ, and if you err like all humans do, you're suddenly a hypocrite for doing so as most unbelievers don't understand that Christians are sinful by nature, too, and just because we believe in Christ it doesn't make our choices perfect; the issue for us, of course, is are we trying to be like the Master or are we still stuck in the world).

4. I prefer to write novel-length fiction hands down, the reason being is I'm long-winded and my stories tend to be too complicated to fit in, say, a mere short tale. Most of my work, novel-wise, is 80,000 words up to as high as 236,000 words.

5. I don't have a particular writing method other than making myself a cup of coffee before each sitting and smoking a cigarette (bad habit, I know, one I'm trying to kick) before I sit down to type. I use that "quiet time" to think about where the story is going next. The most I do in terms of planning ahead is if I get an idea for a cool scene, I'll jot it down. I will only include that scene, however, if the story tells me that that scene should be included. I'm very much a believer in the story knowing what's best and letting it take you where it will instead of me taking it where I think it should go. I've found that my best work comes from me "letting go" and letting the story do all the work. My job is merely to type down what I see in my head as the ideas come.

6. This is a question that really demands a book-length answer. In short, yes. All writers write what they know. For me, I tend to write about circumstances that I've been through albeit changed to suit the course of my story. I've been hurt by other woman prior to getting married and so these feelings of pain and "where was God?" have made it into my earlier work. I've had my share of frustrations with this business and so if I write a story featuring a writer as a character, I get to vent what I think is unfair about this business behind the veil of fiction.

I tend to use my work as a kind of commentary on what I feel is right and wrong with the world. These sorts of themes and ideas just come out almost subconsciously and rarely have I said, "Okay, in this book I want to explore such-and-such a theme." I mean, I have done it but I've also realized that theme is more by accident than on purpose and is something you pick up on when you're doing your subsequent drafts of a manuscript.

7. The same as you hear from everyone else: write a lot and read a lot. Be sure to write every day. You can't *dream* of being a writer. Either you write or you don't. There's no in between.

8. I write in the evenings or super late at night. When working on a project, I do 1500+ words a day, 5-6 days a week. I don't edit while I'm doing the first draft otherwise I'd probably never get past the first chapter. I just spill it all out first then worry about the mess I made later.

I write in my office at home. It used to be that when I was done a book, I'd take it to the Perkins down the road and do my edits there (I always edit longhand), but since getting married and having a kid, now my edits are confined to the bedroom, lying on my back on the bed and editing 50 or so pages per "lying."

9. Not really. All my work takes place in my home city of Winnipeg so I know the place very well. If I'm not sure how to spell a street name but know where it is, during my second or

third draft I'll take the car out for a ride and find out. Likewise with any police procedures. I have no problem walking up to a cop at Tim Horton's and asking him/her about what protocol says they should do in a particular circumstance.

10. Lately, with *Axiom-man*, it's been comic book fans and closet superhero geeks. As to why they enjoy it, that's pretty self-explanatory. As for my more supernatural stuff, namely horror fans or those who enjoy religious tales without in-your-face preaching. Most people (unbelievers) don't have a problem with religiously-themed supernatural horror. They only have a problem when confronted with Gospel.

11. A strong sense of good versus evil, I would say. Though all novels have some kind of "good versus evil" element, my stories tend to be disguised superhero tales when I'm not dealing with men in spandex specifically, and so have a very much clear cut view of the good guy(s) and the bad guy(s). Even my fantasy novel, *The Way of the Fog*, though it doesn't feature guys in tights, it's clearly a superhero novel in a medieval-like setting.

12. It's called *Undeniable* and it's about a man who is captured in communist China and is brutally tortured in the hopes that he'll deny the Lord. The reason I wrote it—and wrote it fairly graphically—was to pose the question both to myself and to the reader: how much would you endure for Christ? It's easy to say, like Peter had, that we'd go with Jesus to the death. But what if you were *actually* faced with it? What if each moment of every day was pure agony? Would you be tempted to deny Him so you could have some relief? Would you keep your eternal perspective at all costs?

I also included a supernatural element to the story as I've always been curious as to what goes on behind the "curtain of the natural." In the story, we get to see the angelic and demonic influence in the torture room and perhaps answer the question as to why God would allow His servants to undergo brutality when He could clearly put a stop to it if He wanted to.

It's a long story, about 11,000 words, about twice what I intended, but—again, listening to the story—that's what it took to make the reader care about the characters undergoing the torture, so much so that the reader him/herself will also feel their pain and so ask themselves if they are truly ready to undergo real and true suffering for Christ or not. And in these last days, that's a serious question we all need to ask ourselves.

In His service,

Stephen OGorman

January 17, 2007

Dear Stephen:

How are you?

Normally I don't look at other creators' ideas. It's a standing policy amongst most, if not all, writers to never look at another's ideas for fear of those ideas somehow leaking into one's subconscious only to later surface in one's own work. However, since my wife speaks highly of you, I'll make an exception. Likewise, and please don't take this the wrong way, your young age is a factor in my decision.

My wife had passed on your summary for *League of Heroes* and I was told you wanted my thoughts. Fair enough. I read your summary and it reads very much like a back story to whatever tale you plan on telling. Which is a good thing, of course. I, too, had to have a back story when it came to Axiom-man and how he received his powers and what may be going on "behind the scenes." Having such a back story is important to any sort of saga as later, when you write the actual tale, it'll add a level of depth to the story that wouldn't be there otherwise.

I won't pretend to be versed in every single superhero story out there, especially when it comes to back stories, so assuming that your idea is an original one and hasn't been done before, I'd say it's a good one and one that you should pursue.

My suggestions are three:

One. You will have to change the title of your story as "League of Heroes" was in use when I did a Google search on it.

Two. The part when you mention that some use their newfound abilities for good but for reasons unexplained. I think you should explain those reasons and why those people decide to use their gifts to help others instead of just helping themselves. A hero without motivation is a useless one. One of the secrets to making a great superhero stems from the fact that the reader/viewer can identify with *why* a hero does what he/she does. So please consider this. Likewise for those who choose to use their powers for evil.

Three. Though you definitely have a good imagination, the writing itself needs work. No worries though as there isn't a writer out there who doesn't need work. Even those topping the bestseller lists aren't "the best" and are always looking for ways to improve their craft (at least the ones I've talked to). And I myself strive to do one better writing-wise with each story outing. The remedy to one's writing ailments is simple: write a lot and read a lot. Practice makes perfect, as the saying goes. And when you're reading a book, pay attention to how the sentences are put together and why they work and why they sometimes don't. Also—though a writer can't be taught *how* to write, but merely guided—a good rule book on writing wouldn't hurt. My suggestion to you would be *The Elements of Style* by William Strunk

Jr. and E.B. White. It's considered by many to be the "bible" of writing.

Feel free to take the above as you will and please only take my criticism as constructive. My suggestions and criticism aren't against you personally. One thing you'll find, if you get heavy into this business, is that criticism comes hard and fast with this game and if you don't develop a thick skin, you'll be out of the race before you even begin. So keep at it and keep typing. If you work hard on your skills now, by the time you reach manhood you'll be a literary force to be reckoned with.

I hope you found the above both encouraging and useful.

Your friend,

Susan Kirkland

January 23, 2007

Dear Susan:

Thrilled to hear you loved *Axiom-man.* And thanks again for wishing to review it for your newspaper. I'm assuming it's for the *Calhoun Times*, then?

Thanks, as well, for permission to lift a sentence or two for a blurb. It'll be "whatever you say," S.M. Kirkland, *Calhoun Times*, if that's all right (please advise if you wish to see it changed to something else).

Regarding where to mail me a copy of the review when it's available, sending it my email address is fine. For snail mail, please send to:

A.P. Fuchs
****
Winnipeg, MB
****
Canada

To answer your question about the sequel, I've got roughly 11-12,000 words to go (assuming it goes as I presently have it in mind, but with novels, you never know, right?), so I'm expecting *Axiom-man II* will be out in June sometime. I'll make an official announcement and also disclose the official title of the second book as I near publication.

As a side note, if you're looking for other good independent superhero novels, may I recommend the following:

The Wraith by Frank Dirscherl
Valley of Evil (also a Wraith novel) by Frank Dirscherl
Rush and the Grey Fox by Jon Klement
Rush and the Grey Fox: Ready to Rumble (eBook) by Jon Klement
Knight Seeker by Eric Cooper
The Shadow Fox Chronicles Part 1 by Julie Staples

Anyway, thanks again for your interest in *Axiom-man.* If you wish to keep up-to-date with the character, please visit axiomman.blogspot.com for all the latest info.

In His service,

Darryl Sloan

March 7, 2007

Dear Darryl:

Yesterday afternoon I finished reading *Chion,* which was a marked improvement over *Ulterior.* That's not to say *Ulterior* was terrible by any means. I already told you I really enjoyed it, but some of the bumps and bruises *Ulterior* carried were absent in *Chion.*

As I read it, I marked a few passages and/or circumstances which I found particularly appealing and/or interesting.

They are:

Page 13: Jamie having visions of snipers hiding around the school and the neighboring houses as a possible reason for the school's lockdown. This resonated with me because I was a kid with an overactive imagination and always had ideas of happenings larger than life that my teachers and parents weren't telling me. Further, when one is a kid, it is much easier to concoct ideas and/or visions in the mind's eye than it is when you're an adult. I'm a firm believer that a person is given a fireball of imagination when they are born, but as time wears on, so does that fireball wear down and unless one adds fuel to the fire, eventually it will puff out and a person will be condemned to a life in the real world without the blessed, and sometimes much-needed, escape of the imagination. This is why, I suspect, that creative people and "regular" people often collide in their thinking and approach to life. Creative people always ask the "what if" question about things whereas your average person approaches circumstances as they are with practicality, and rarely, if ever, venture outside the box in an attempt to react and/or address a specific circumstance. Though, of course, addressing things in the realm of reality is crucial, to limit oneself to what "everybody else does" or "this is what normal people do to remedy this" is a terrible mistake. There is more than one way to skin a cat, as the saying goes. Reading about Jamie's vision of snipers brought me back to my youth and reminded me of the power an imagination can have.

Page 37: Jamie reflecting on the unfortunate truth that when it comes to high-stakes/cataclysmic circumstances, people respond to God in one of two ways: they either cry out against Him or turn to Him for comfort. I found your inclusion of the statement in the book particularly fitting for the time of history we live in, namely one where acts of God are happening on a daily basis and in extremes that humanity has not seen since the beginning of its history. Though these disasters are to be expected and, frankly, do not surprise me anymore, the fact that God comes up in people's minds after the event rings true, whether they are authentic believers in Him or not. Most people, it seems, become *temporal* believers in Him after a calamity strikes. After all, humanity is known for always wanting to find a scapegoat when trial strikes and who better to blame than God, right? The missing ingredient in this thinking, of course, is the forgetfulness that God can come in and do as He pleases when He pleases, and this includes allowing and/or sending a disaster upon the earth. We tend to forget that He is in charge and has every right to do as He sees fit with His creation, whether that be people themselves or the nature He has created. Thankfully, though, and as you pointed out, these horrible disasters also produce a good side effect, and that is the turning of hearts toward Him. And, I suspect, these disasters, as tragic as they are, are the only way to get certain people's attention. Most people need something to go wrong beyond their control in order for them to look up. If they could control it, they could either blame themselves (though people hate doing that) or blame others. But when something occurs that could only come from something other than human, then they have no choice but address the One other Person who could have caused it. It's my prayer that in the days and months ahead, when further disasters strike, lives will be changed as a result and people will seek the Lord with all their heart even though they may not understand why the tragedy occurred.

Page 45: Jamie's comment on the built-in need for a human being to want to live. Most folks would chalk this up as being mere survival instinct, but you and I know it reaches much further than that. Though I'm sure it was part of God's design for us to want to live, I also know that humanity's need to live despite trial or despite bad medical news is His safety mechanism in us to help us persevere instead of giving up. It's a preservation thing. I also think that such a mechanism, though physical, also reaches into the spiritual in that we all have that God-shaped void within us, the void we try and fill with booze and drugs and sex and money and whatnot before we know the Lord. The desire to live goes beyond the physical; most people believe in some sort of afterlife. The very idea of dying and then kaput terrifies most because it is hard to imagine an existence where existence isn't even present at all. Unfortunately, what has happened is that humanity's spiritual survival instinct has been numbed down to pretty much nothing due to sin and the evil climate we live in, in the year 2007. Sin numbs feeling; truth brings it back. And it's this numbing which forbids some to not seek anything *but* the temporal, to not look outside the physical into a realm which is all too real in spite of a part of them wondering "what's out there."

Page 60: The comment of the drum beat being played with the skill of a chimpanzee made me smile. Just wanted to point that out.

Page 71: After the shooting incident and the students lose faith in the adult world. It is true that kids believe adults to be almost immortal and all-powerful, capable of all things that are right and true and just. I know for myself, growing up, I relied heavily on my teachers and believed with all my heart that everything they told me both academically and by way of just simple advice was 100% true. Same with my parents. Kids have the preconceived notion that grown ups have it all figured out, but it's not until those same kids grow up do they realize just how much their parents or teachers were winging it or faking it. I'm tasting that for myself now. When I was younger, I thought that by the time I reached my age I'd have life pretty much figured out, I'd be wise and know all things just like my folks. Now that I'm here, I realize how far from that truth that really is and, just like my folks, I'm figuring it out as I go along and that life truly is a learning process, one that isn't even complete by the time you die. I don't know when the shift in my perception changed, when I had that revelation, but probably after I got married was when it hit home the hardest.

Page 124: Jamie leaving Mr. Parka and Mr. Leather to die. Talk about a kill-or-be-killed circumstance. I mean, really, what would you do if faced with that choice? This is something I personally haven't yet decided upon. I honestly can't imagine myself being so selfish as to do what it takes to preserve my life at the cost of another, and yet if that occasion ever occurred, how much would the panic and the aforementioned survival instinct dictate my actions. I'm sure for you that writing that scene was difficult. It seems to me Jamie, to a large degree, isn't just a mere character on a page but an extension of yourself. The whole "write what you know" thing. And when penning it you would have had to take into account what *Jamie* would do but, since you were living the scene with Jamie and Tara, what *you* would also do if it came down to it. I'm not saying you'd allow others to perish to save your own skin, but I'm sure you must have paused from the keyboard and seriously wondered how you'd personally tackle this while also keeping in mind where the story was going and what else needed to be accomplished in the tale to reach an acceptable resolution.

Page 131: Tara and Jamie's tender moment in the boat's cabin. The need those two had for each other after all they had been through. Man, good stuff. Especially that line when Tara tells him to just keep kissing her. Even Jamie felt it himself—all the stuff they've been through didn't seem to matter while he held her. It's interesting how another person can have that affect on someone. I've been there. And especially more so since I've been married. There have been times when things have gone so, so wrong that it seemed as if hope was completely lost, but all it took was the closeness of my wife and suddenly the storm calmed.

Page 140: Tara commenting on Jamie about to steal that moped. Though she was just joking, Jamie made a good point about her worrying about the theft even though the day before he killed a couple people. Some would say, "Ah, at least he's not killing anyone *again.*" Others would say, "Well, because they need the moped to survive, stealing is okay." And yet others would say, "Life or death, stealing is wrong." Again, an interesting dilemma. There's the world's view on this (one that, evidently, Jamie shares), and then God's view on it. It's the age-old question of when is it all right to break God's laws? The answer, of course, is never. Yet people still keep trying to find a way and come up with excuses. I just thought this part was interesting because Jamie, though already racked with guilt over the murders, still decided to commit yet another crime all in the name of survival. Though his tears suggested he knew better, by him stealing, it conveyed he was already on his way down a slippery slope.

In the end, yes, a very good story, one which I enjoyed. I found the ending a bit too Disney-like, but that could just be me.

I hope you have another novel coming up soon as I really don't want to wait 5 more years till the next one.

Sincerely,

Dave Sim

March 13, 2007

Dear Dave:

How have you been? The last I wrote you was July, 2006, so quite sometime ago. Man, has it been that long? Guess so.

Anyway...

I'm about 30 pages away from completing *Collected Letters 2004*. I would have been done much sooner but had misplaced the book for several months and finally recovered it about a week ago. Very intriguing material all around. One thing that kept popping up in your letters was the question of when/if the mail would taper off and you'd finally have some actual retirement time. Aside from this letter taking up space in your mailbox, has your letter-answering load lightened since, say, May of 2004? I know it hasn't dropped off altogether since you now post at *Dave Sim's Blogandmail* (speaking of which, is that where I should find a reply to this letter, if you do reply? I must admit, I don't check the blog all that often, namely due to there not being enough hours in the day to read through everything).

Things have been going well over on my end. Just the other week my wife and I found out we're pregnant with our second child. We'll find out within the next couple of weeks the actual due date but we're estimating it to be somewhere between late October to early November. This also means that we'll begin house hunting sometime in May to allow room for the newest addition to the family.

On the self-publishing front, I crossed a milestone in my career on September 29, 2006, when I released my independent superhero novel entitled, *Axiom-man*, who was a character I created back in my high school drawing days and finally, after all these years, decided to actually do something with him other than fantasize heroic tales about him in my head. The reason the release was a milestone was because of the wonderful media attention—not to mention sales—that resulted due to the character being Winnipeg's own superhero. TV, Radio, Newspaper—very exciting as most self-published authors are usually swept under the rug because they're not "real" publishers. What I always found interesting about that argument was that, in the end, the reader doesn't care if you've been published by a "real" publisher or not. They just care about getting a good story.

At the beginning of March, the first draft of the sequel was completed, coming in at about 119,000 words, which is nearly double the length of its predecessor. It's called *Axiom-man: Doorway of Darkness* and takes place right where the first one left off. This second book is planned to be released end of July along with a short novella called *Axiom-man Episode #0: First Night Out* which chronicles, you guessed it, his first night out. The Axiom-man "episode" series is there for those stories I wish to tell that aren't large enough scale-wise to warrant a full 80,000+ words to make it a "feature." I'm viewing them more like half hour cartoon episodes ala *Batman: The Animated Series*, where, though there's a couple of plotlines going on, it's more light-hearted and simple compared to the depths of character and story I can get into with a full-length novel. (For example, book two carries five plotlines.)

Which brings me to stating what an honor it will be for our two characters to stand side by side in 2008's *War of the Independents*, which, I understand, Cerebus will be participating in. I think the project will do well and the premise of the mini series sounds interesting. We'll see. I trust Scott Lobdell, who is writing the project.

I wanted to ask you about how you went about writing and drawing the *Cerebus* storyline? That is, how you planned out the 25-or-so issues for a particular arc and what a day in the life of

Dave Sim was like? It's one thing if a person was only the artist or writer on a series. Pretty straight forward in regards to their day-to-day tasks. But when you couple a few creative tasks together, time management is critical. I love hearing about how other artists approach their craft—habits, routines, etc.—regardless of medium so, please, spill your guts as I'm all ears.

Hope to hear from you.

Take care.

Sincerely,

Richard Pulfer

March 30, 2007

Dear Richard:

Sorry for the late reply. Been a harrowing couple of days.

As previously mentioned, yes, my attitude for approaching other writers for blurbs has always been, "The worst they could do is say no."

In terms of "protocol," a letter to them might read (and, honestly, it's varied from writer to writer, but the gist is the same):

Dear Mr./Ms. Author:

My name is My Name and I'm in the process of gathering blurbs for my novel/comic, My Book.

Brief synopsis:

Yadda yadda yadda (keep it very brief, like 3-5 sentences)

Having read your novel/comic, His/Her Book—which I loved/liked/enjoyed/etc., by the way—I'd very much be honored if you'd consider reviewing my story for endorsement. Please note that should you agree, you're under no obligation to endorse the material if you don't enjoy it for whatever reason. I just kindly request you please let me know so I'm not left wondering/waiting.

Thank you for your time and consideration. I look forward to your reply.

Sincerely,

Your Name

And there you go. No real formula, but I keep my letters very professional and formal. Should the author and I become friends, then I alter my tone according to the closeness of our friendship.

That's pretty much it. I hope the above helps.

Good to hear from you again.

In His service,

Amber Delisle-Corps

April 24, 2007

Dear Amber:

Thank you for all the kind words. I'm happy you enjoyed *A Stranger Dead*, *A Red Dark Night* and *The Way of the Fog.*

Regarding *Parasitic Sands*, the book is an anthology with stories by several authors, with me being one of them. My story is called *Beneath the Sand*, which is a tale about a guy who wakes up buried alive at a beach at night. It's horror, but not as fantastical (in other words, your more basic horror) as *A Red Dark Night* or *The Way of the Fog*. The book, unfortunately, and so far as I'm aware, is available online only, at lulu.com (the link is: http://www.lulu.com/content/643131). Thanks in advance if you check it out.

No problem on not currently being a superhero fan. For *Axiom-man*, I basically tell folks that if they like Superman, Spider-man or Batman, then they'll like Axiom-man as he's kind of a mix of all three. This one is carried in bookstores and, last I heard, Chapters at Polo Park had a display for it on the top floor in the fantasy/sci-fi/horror section. The sequel to this story is due out July 27, 2007.

I'm sorry to hear about your recent experience with your boss and other "fanatic" Christian friends. (Though I'm not sure what you mean by "fanatic" as, to me, a Christian *should* be a fanatic, that is, a fanatic about Jesus Christ.) And, no, you didn't offend me by any means. If you'd like to share your experience(s) with me, my door's open and all will be kept confidential. However—and I could be way off here—was their fanaticism in the area of "being judgmental"? If so, I have a blog entry I posted the other day at http://coscomentertainment.blogspot.com and it deals with just that issue (and, if this is the case, I'm on your side because Christians should *not* be judgmental).

Regarding the *Ark of Light* series, to be honest, I'm not 100% sure what's going to happen with that. I know of some folks who are eagerly awaiting *The Way of the Fog* sequel (which, at present, is about 1/3 done), but some things have recently happened on my end in regards to the series and I don't know if I'll be pursuing it anymore. I'm awaiting confirmation from the Lord in regards to the future of the series (no sense in doing it if He doesn't want me to).

At present, my main area of focus writing-wise is the Axiom-man saga. I just finished *Axiom-man Episode #0: First Night Out*, which is a prequel/sequel (that label will make sense if you read it) to the first book. *Episode #0*, a novella, will be co-released with book two this summer. I plan on getting into *Episode #1* shortly as my next project, though I may do a short story first. We'll see.

Thanks for contacting me.

Sincerely,

Greg Mitchell

June 25, 2007

Dear Greg:

Thanks for writing and congratulations on the recent release of your book, *The Coming Evil*.

Getting the word out is one of the biggest hurdles an author has to overcome. Most of us are just writers, not promoters, but as is the publishing climate these days, most of the promo work (unless you're a publisher's big seller) falls on the author, and more and more authors are spending most, if not all, of their advance just on the promotional side of things. And for those who chose to self-publish, getting the word out is even harder because then you have to work against the prejudices of the bookstores against self-published books, namely POD ones (believe me, I know). And the problem most do-it-yourselfers face is promoting their book on a shoestring or even non-existent budget.

Here's my turn for a plug: I wrote a book called *Book Marketing for the Financially-challenged Author*. The Lost Genre Guild recently bought a bunch of copies and distributed them to those part of the *Light at the Edge of Darkness* anthology. (I have a story in there called *Undeniable*; you should definitely check out the collection as it's pure Christian spec-fic.) My marketing book is basically a primer on getting the word out about your novel and how to do it for, all told, the cost of a meal.

I agree. Taking a stand against is evil is a standard "superhero" thing (even the all-too-used anti-hero still fights evil), but it could also be a "horror" thing, too, depending on how you play your cards. I mean, look at Frank Peretti. Monster/supernatural stories all around, but the ultimate battle between Good and Evil is played out in his books: Jesus versus the Devil.

Thanks again for writing. God bless you in your publishing journey. May His will be done.

The door's open anytime.

Best,

Joel Comiskey

July 18, 2007

Dear Joel:

Forgive me for my late reply. It's been hectic around the Coscom Entertainment office these past couple of weeks as I gear up for the two new Axiom-man releases coming out on July 27. I've also been swamped recording and promoting the *Axiom-man* Podcast novel (see http://www.apfuchs.com/podcast.html).

So, onto printer stuff:

Since publishing my work via my own label, I've used POD straight through. Lots of ups and downs along the way. I learned what to do and what not to do and I'm *still* learning.

I've used Lightning Source since day one because I haven't yet found a digital printer here in Canada that is affordable. And there is yet to be one that offers a distribution package of some kind (from what I know).

With my *Axiom-man* series, I'll do a short run for all my direct and local sales, then use Lightning's distribution system for all my online stuff and for whoever wants to order my books through brick and mortar stores in the States or overseas (UK). The only real drawback for me is getting my books in over the border as I get hit with Customs and GST charges which, depending on the size of my order, can range from $40-100. Granted, when all the numbers are crunched, I still come out on top, but if I could save that $40-100, I would.

Now, because our dollars are so similar, it might be in my best interest to find a printer either locally or a province or two over for my short run stuff and maybe get them to do a price match of some kind. The only thing holding me back from that idea, so far, is having to pay the setup fee twice: one for Lightning, the other for whatever printer I might end up with.

Lightning's distribution services is only $12 a year and that's for both US and UK distribution. Well, "wholesale listings," technically, but regardless, if you make $4-6 per book after discounts, you only need to sell 2 or 3 and you've made your $12 back. It's worth it, plus they handle the fulfillment side of things so you just have to market the book(s) then collect.

Great to know there's another believer on the board. Feels like we're a dwindling bunch these days. (To be expected, however, given Paul's foretelling of the apostasy in these last days.) As a side note, I'm writing the sermons for my church this month. We're doing a four-parter on prophecy and parts one and two are up on my blog at http://coscomentertainment.blogspot.com Parts three and four will be posted over the next two weeks. Feel free to give them a read when you have a moment.

Thanks for writing.

For His Glory,

Richard Burley

July 29, 2007

Dear Richard:

Thanks for your email on July 26.

Normally I'm pretty diligent with replies but this past weekend was "launch" weekend for me as on July 27 *Doorway of Darkness* and *Episode No. 0: First Night Out* were released, and my time was spent launching those books on the web and at a couple of bookstores this past weekend.

I apologize for the delay in response.

On to your email:

Thank you for the kind words regarding the Axiom-man podcast. I'm glad I got you hooked. And thank you even more for going out of your way to post a blog entry about it. I read it and it made me smile.

More audio files are available (and more are being produced). Episode 8 should be up right after I write you. It's recorded and I'm just giving it the final proof before posting it. (Got a new sound equalizer so sound quality should improve from now on.) New episodes will be released every Friday until the story is done. 23 episodes total. Be sure to use the subscribe link on the website so you don't miss an episode.

What will happen when Axiom-man encounters his first supervillain? Read and find out, as Robert Jordan says.

Your criticism on "missing a good and solid defensive power," well, all I'll say is what I said above, "Read and find out." There's a reason why, at first, Axiom-man seems a little unsure as to what to do and also why sometimes crooks land a shot or two on him. One of them is simply: that's real life. I've never been a fan of the hero who walks in, beats the bad guys with no effort, then walks out. Real fights don't happen that way so why should they in superhero stories? And the second reason is he doesn't have any formal combat training, like Kung Fu or Tae Kwon Do. He's just a guy who received powers and tried to do the right thing with them (there's more to it than that, but you get the idea). Will he receive formal training? Again, read and find out.

I also hope, too, that God will use this tale for Jesus. The Axiom-man series isn't meant to be "Christian fiction," in the conventional sense. But it is most definitely told from a Christian worldview. However, I won't take the Bible and wrap a superhero story around it then whack people over the head with it. The problem with Christian fiction, in my opinion (and though I do read some), is that it really is catered to Christians and Christians only, for the most part. It's basically the Bible with a story around it. Which is fine (I'm not opposed to the Bible, of course), but I think the author suddenly only limits his/her audience to believers and believers only that way. What I'm hoping to do with the Axiom-man series is reach both believers and unbelievers alike (ala C.S. Lewis or J.R.R. Tolkien). I'm not putting my writing on par with theirs—few can—but their audience is both Christian and non-Christian. Will Christianity play a part in the Axiom-man storyline? For sure. Will it occupy every single page? Nope. And not out of "shame" or anything silly like that. Again, I don't want Joe Unbeliever reading it then chucking it across the room because the Bible is preached on every page. (And in these Last Days, unbelievers will be growing even more opposed to the Gospel unlike ever before so I don't want to lose anyone while I'm still on Earth; I'm a prophecy nut, by the way.)

For me, so far as I know, Axiom-man is one of the first, if not THE first, Christian superhero story. There are others, but it's your usual deal of some guy with a cross on his chest battling demons in a standard spiritual warfare way. I'd like to say more but then I'd be giving away future plotlines that may or may not come to fruition. All I'll say is Axiom-man will be, hopefully, something new and fresh both secularly and Christian-wise as the storyline progresses.

Thank you in advance if you pick up the books. They're all self-contained tales but all part of a single story. The first three (*Axiom-man*, *Doorway of Darkness* and *First Night Out*) constitute the first story arc of the series. Episode No. 1 (presently untitled) will be out early 2008 with book 3 (untitled) due in the fall of 2008. (The books are written as "feature films" whereas the episodes are more like half-hour cartoon shows.)

Regarding Axiom-man versus the Cthulhu monster, though I appreciate your enthusiasm for it, it would be unfair to Permuted Press for me to share that story, which is on submission for acceptance with them, with you. Just ethics, is all. Sorry.

Thanks again for dropping me a line.

Sincerely,

Fehlandt

August 30, 2007

Dear Fehlandt:

Thanks for your note from August 18.

You certainly finished off *Doorway of Darkness* quickly, considering it's a much bigger book than *Axiom-man*. I'm glad you liked it.

Unfortunately you'll have to wait a bit for the next installment. Book 3 isn't scheduled till September of 2008. However, Episode No. 1 will be out May or June of 2008, so that'll be a little something to tide you over. Neither is written yet though I did start book 3 last night and wrote the first 1790 words. All I can really tell you about it are three things: 1) there'll be a new villain, 2) it takes place during winter, and 3) it'll continue the storyline from book 2 though it takes place several months after those events. As of now, the Episode No. 1 story will tie into it and I'll be writing that while I wait for the book 3 manuscript to cool down once it's completed.

The episode series is meant to be read alongside the main sequence books, the plan being a back-and-forth between the two formats (i.e. main sequence book, episode, main sequence book, episode, etc.), all one storyline.

I heard you played your last city game of the season the other night. Any more games on the horizon or are you done till the Goldeyes take the field next year?

Thanks again for writing. Would have written you back sooner but I was out of town last week in Saskatoon doing a few book signings and visiting with friends and family.

For His Glory,

Sean Simmons

October 10, 2007

Dear Sean:

Below are my answers for WPJ.

How long have you been writing?

Since June, 2000. I got into it writing comic book scripts for guys I went to animation school with, and when the school didn't deliver on what they were supposed to teach us, I switched mediums because I fell in love with writing stories instead of drawing them.

What was your first novel?

After writing comics, I did a couple short stories then began work on a serial short story, which I planned to be five or six parts long. Instead, when I finished the tale, it wound up being the prologue to my first novel, *A Stranger Dead.*

Who's your favorite Superhero?

I thought you said I'd have to think on some of these? My favorite superhero's Axiom-man, of course!

Other than Axiom-man, who's your favorite superhero?

Well, okay, I'll tell you. I'm a Superman guy, through and through. He comes first. Always has. Then after him are Nightwing, Batman and Spider-man.

Quickly now: Books or Comics?

Manga. So Japanese comics.

Which makes a better film, a Book or a Comic?

Comics. Easy. If done properly. Comics are basically just storyboards broken down into 22-page blocks, stapled together. For the most part, I've enjoyed the comic book films of recent years (*Batman Begins*, *Spider-man* 1-3, the first 2 *X-Men* flicks (the third was more a bookend than a movie), *V for Vendetta*, etc.). Some not so much (*Superman Returns*, *Hulk*).

Books, based on all the adaptations I've seen, fall short 9 times out of 10. Books—there's so much more story. They're longer, more complicated. To accurately translate a book to film 100%, the movie would have to be a minimum of 6 hours (like *The Stand*, which was brilliant), but, of course, Hollywood can't do that because the theatres couldn't handle a movie of that length due to the other stuff they need to show, so there's always concessions when filming a book, usually resulting in cutting out a good chunk of it or combining characters into one, etc.

Do you enjoy collaborating?

Ha! When I have to. Actually, yeah, I enjoy it. It's a good chance for me to stretch creatively and also to relearn teamwork since I'm very much a do-it-yourselfer when it comes to publishing. And being a complete do-it-yourself can also be a dangerous thing because sometimes it becomes "Your way or bust" when what you really need is a slap in the face from someone else telling you where you're succeeding and where you're failing. Thank goodness for grumpy comic artists to say, "Here's what I think..."

Of all the cities in the world, why Winnipeg?

When Axiom-man showed up in the city, I was just as surprised as anyone. I mean, really, Winnipeg? Why not one of the big cities? That question stuck with me for the longest time until one day I was nearly rundown by some dude with too much attitude and a big car, and out of nowhere this streak of blue lifts me out of harms way and sets me down to safety beside the road.

It was Axiom-man.

At first I thought I'd see him that one time and that'd be it, but every time he patrols my neighborhood, and if I'm out and about, he'll fly down and say hello. Sometimes we talk, and he once told me he likes it here in Winnipeg because he's still getting his boots wet in this whole crimefighting gig and to go to a city with millions of people like New York or Toronto or Chicago—he wouldn't be comfortable with that. Not yet. Too much at stake if he messes up. And I have to agree. He's a better service to us here in the 'Peg by taking on what he can handle and not trying to play it tough by selling out to a bustling metropolis just for the sake of size or, even, prestige.

Do you really think Winnipeg needs a superhero? Don't you think it was getting along fine without one?

Since Axiom-man's been on the scene, crime's dropped to, last I heard, 35% of what it used to be, so obviously he's making a difference. A *huge* difference. Cops can go only go so far, do so much. He gets in where they can't, pulls through where they fall short. Personally, I feel much safer knowing he's out there, watching over me.

Magic Man is a REAL bad guy. Who, if anyone, inspired him?

That's the problem with the Magic Man. Word is no one's really talked to him. He's never been caught. Only a rumor as to who he is floats around, but even then it might not be accurate.

Something about a little boy and a weird relationship with his mother. Even when Axiom-man encountered him—so Axiom-man later told me—the Magic Man never went on in some supervillain diatribe about his past. He remains a mystery and probably one best kept closed. The guy's too twisted. I get sick just thinking about what he does to people. I couldn't stomach *Saw III* and according to the papers, what the Magic Man does makes Jigsaw look like Bob the Builder. The guy's a maniac. Sick, sadistic and has a thing for surgically-altering others. I just hope one day Axiom-man takes him down. Maybe then we'll learn some answers as to who he is and where he came from. Until then, lock the doors, though I've heard that doesn't really help either.

Thankfully, Axiom-man's out there looking out for us.

Marco Moreira

January 2, 2008

Dear Marco:

Thanks for taking the time to write to me. I apologize for the delay in reply but the Holiday Season got the best of me, and my family and I were running over the place.

I also want to thank you for such a wonderful letter. It's always nice when someone drops me a note and says they enjoyed *Axiom-man*.

Thinking back, I do remember you. Kind of a hazy image but I remember you picking up the first two installments of the series.

I'm the same as you regarding the hero "keeping clean" despite whatever entanglements they find themselves in. To me, I find it real hard to suspend disbelief when a superpowered situation arises that requires superpowered help, and then suddenly the hero appears and solves everything without breaking a sweat. One of the things I'm trying to capture with the Axiom-man books is simply, "It wouldn't be that easy, folks, if this stuff really happened."

What you've read thus far is pretty much the intro stuff, a sort of "here's everybody" kind of thing. All origin stuff. Things get pretty intense from here on out, starting with *Doorway of Darkness* and the current comic book, *Of Magic and Men*. There is some origin stuff, too, in *Doorway of Darkness*. The first novel answered the "how" of Gabriel getting his powers. *Doorway of Darkness* answers the "why." And Redsaw's a whole lot meaner, by the way, now that he's turned to evil.

So once again, thanks for your note. I look forward to your thoughts on *Doorway of Darkness* once you check it out (Coles still has copies). Also, if you'd like, feel free to write a review of *Axiom-man* and/or *First Night Out* at Amazon.com/ca, should the mood strike you. It's always enjoyable to see what people think of the character, good, bad or ugly.

More Axiom-man stuff coming your way this year (another episode and another full-length novel), so keep watching the skies (or the website).

Sincerely,

Eric Lernould

July 4, 2012

Dear Eric:

I'm glad you're enjoying the *Axiom-man* webcomic. I hope the upcoming stories interest you just as much. Likewise, if you haven't already, consider picking up the novels as, continuity-wise, they take place before the comic series.

To be honest, I'm relatively new to the webcomic community, but am no stranger to publishing, the arts, etc. Comics were my original plan of career choice until my dreams got derailed due to life circumstances and an animation school that didn't deliver on its curriculum. However, now that I'm back into making comics regularly, it's like coming home after taking a few detours along the way.

That said, the current comic book climate is much, much different than it was back when I was aiming for a career in the field, aspirations starting in either 1994 or 1995 (have to check my earliest drawings to verify). At the same time, though, thanks to being involved in publishing since 2003, I've been able to witness trends and technology evolution that is clearly influencing my comic book goals of today.

We're obviously living in a tech-driven society where more and more entertainment—pick your medium—will be delivered via a computer or tablet—probably 99% tablets in the near future—and right now the comic biz is sitting on the ground floor, wondering which button will get the elevator to go up.

Webcomics, to me—and the current webcomic model, especially—are very limited as a means to create a career from. If that's your goal, other avenues to earn money will have to be explored. If this is just a hobby thing, then you're pretty much set.

One thing I did notice on the Kickstarter page is no print option was offered as one of the rewards. It would be great if you could collect the strips at the end of each season and offer them for sale as a means to further fund the comic. Likewise, I enjoy picking up collections or single issues of indie comics that catch my interest.

If some tips are required, my suggestions are to a) get a backlog three-to-four weeks' worth of strips before posting the first one and get yourself some lead time in case you get sick, computer melts down, etc., b) if you say you're going to post on a certain day(s), then post on that day(s). Consistency is everything in webcomics based on those I've talked to and other reading I've done, c) hope for the comic to be a huge success but understand usually it starts off slow as you build an audience.

But to tie in to what I said above about your goal(s) with this thing, this is the first question I ask any artist or writer who wants to start putting out their material: what IS your goal with this? You need to define what it is you're after otherwise you won't have a destination never mind even a starting point. Is this for fun? A part time job? Full time? Important questions to answer.

And stop calling yourself an "aspiring cartoonist." If you're cartooning regularly, you're a cartoonist. If you're not, then, okay, you're still "aspiring."

Hope the above helps.

Best,

Dave Sim

August 23, 2012

Dear Dave:

How have you been? Not sure if you remember me from time's past, but you and I corresponded a handful of times back between 2006-07, the topic of our conversation being the "gray stuff" of society, its detriments, etc., and we also touched on self-publishing. (I'm the dude who self-publishes his novels—now comics, too—the main series being *The Axiom-man Saga*, which is a cross-medium superhero story penned by a single creator. Thus far there are two novels, novellas, three short stories, three comics, which the fourth comic almost done likewise the third full novel.)

Not sure if that was a good refresher or not, but hopefully it rings at least one bell, even if ever so quietly.

Apologies in advance for any run-on sentences in this note. Fatigue is a factor these days.

Unless I got my information wrong, I heard you don't correspond with readers anymore, or if you do, it's a select few. Hope you include in me in that bunch as our prior correspondence means a great deal to me.

I've gotten up to *Flight* in the Cerebus storyline. Enjoyed it all the way thus far. *Women* is next and is in my shopping cart at Amazon.ca (which is where I buy most of my books, graphic novels and movies as the price there is 9 times out of 10 cheaper than the stores and if you spend $25 or more, you get free shipping).

A lot has changed since I last wrote you. We had that kid that I mentioned back in my last letter. He's going to be 5 in October. His brother, 7, and him see me write and draw stories all day as my career so I'm pleased to see them already trying their hand at comics. In fact, the 7-year-old has produced three 10-or-so-page minicomics thus far. Well, "mini" in terms of length, but not so mini as we've been stapling 8.5" x 11" pages together then giving them to him to fill in. Regardless, cool stuff as I view comic books as an important part of life given the greatness of the medium or, as Warren Ellis's book describes them in his book's title, *Do Anything*. He's got a fascinating blog, by the way. Some of what he posts is just junk from the Internet, but he does post essays on the current state of the comics medium, the potential of webcomics and where he sees comics and technology colliding both presently and in years to come. He also points the way to other essayists on the subject.

A note of thanks:

As always, I nod my head to you for self-publishing comics motivation. More particularly, having seen the way—and am continuing to learn about—how you put out *Cerebus*, *Cerebus Archive* and *Glamourpuss*, I was inspired to just get on with putting out my *Axiom-man* comics series. Having been active in publishing books—including a couple graphic novels and a few comics—for about 8 years, the timing seemed right given that, due to technological advances, eReading becoming more and more popular, the crazy improvements in digital book production (of which my company, Coscom Entertainment, is based upon)—the comic book model I'm embarking on is pretty much the same as the books'. Not that the two mediums are interchangeable, albeit they are pretty close once the comic book gets to the graphic novel stage.

Based on the research I've done and, it seems, you've experienced due to the cancellation of both *Glamourpuss* and *Cerebus Archive*—sad news on both accounts though I understand the reasons you gave at the *A Moment of Cerebus* Blog—the periodical side of the comics biz, at least for indies, is on the way out, in terms of a sustainable business model upon which to build one's livelihood for a fulltime comics career.

I check in with Terry Moore's blog every other day and a few months back he talked about periodical sales and his current title, *Rachel Rising*, does about 700 copies a month. (See www.terrymooreart.com/?p=1793 ; though the site says 780 were on Diamond's reorder, I basing my guess on the principle that, at least until issue 7 or so, sales decline until plateauing with the hopes of growing after that. Feel free to comment on that info, by the way, as I'm recalling something I read a long time ago on the sales for the average comics title. The article basically said that orders for a number one are high, then number two are 50% of that, then number three 50% of that, then 50% of that and so on until issues 6 or 7, then those who stuck with you that long are pretty much the readers you can count on.) Throw in Diamond's required steep discount and that doesn't leave much for printing the next issue and the supplies required never mind paying the rent.

Anyway, times for self-publishing comics have certainly changed since *Cerebus* started back in 1977. Even since I looked at self-publishing comics via the traditional model back in 1998-99, actually.

Here is my current model. I'm open to any feedback and/or suggestions and/or "what you're doing is crazy" comments.

Since my company is web-based, with 95% of books ordered being online (whether for print or eBooks), the remaining 5% sold at conventions and booksignings, and since I've been able to sustain a living for close to three years based on that, and given the state of tech these days, I think I'm onto something.

Though I've slipped recently due to a major burn-out but am now getting back on track, I agree that, as you've stated—can't remember where—that when folks ask you for the secret to *Cerebus*'s success, you said keeping the book on time is the reason. I believe you. On-time books keep readers interested, give them their fix at regular intervals, and, assuming the sales are there, enables the creator to maintain a steady level of interest as he can sink all his time into his book instead of dividing the comic against a day job.

My model:

1.) Release the book on time in print, electronic download, and twice a week post a page from the comic on Mondays and Thursdays (see www.axiom-man.com). The reason for the webcomic is to raise awareness of the character to help feed print sales and downloads, likewise, if folks like what they read, they will be apt to pick up one or more of my novels.

2.) Forego Diamond for the print periodicals. Due to finances, discounts and such, I'm opting out of Diamond Distribution for the monthly book, instead releasing the copies of the comic for direct sale, short-running each issue at 300 copies. This cost enables me to keep the price low on the book and still make close to a buck an issue. Direct sales include direct ordering, conventions, booksignings, and trunk-of-the-car sales.

3.) Release each print issue through Ka-Blam.com (which is like Comix Press), and utilize their print and digital storefront at Indyplanet.com and Indyplanetdigital.com respectively.

4.) Release each issue in digital format through as many channels as possible (Kindle, Nook, iPad et al.), treating each download as if they are the print counterpart. A sale's a sale, after all.

5.) Once a particular story arc is complete, collected into a graphic novel. Also, ala Mike Mignola, include a bonus story to set the graphic novel apart from the periodical book.

6.) Use Diamond for graphic novel distribution.

7.) Use my printer's amazing distribution system to make the graphic novel available to all the online hotspots like Amazon.com and its sister sites, Barnes and Noble.com, and others. Also offer for direct sale, whether by order, conventions, booksignings, trunk-of-the-car sales, etc.

8.) Offer the graphic novel at a fair price for digital download via all the same channels the periodical was. Perhaps offer the same direct as long as I can ensure proper shopping cart procedure and security through services out there that specialize in online digital product ordering.

Part of being a one-man-band, as you know, is time management as it would be all too easy to turn the running of the company into the fulltime job and not the creating of comics. All of what I mentioned above—aside from direct sales—is based on the do-the-work-once-than-don't-worry-about-it model I've been using for eight years. This then frees up time for creating, marketing, and personal time with family. Might even be time for sleep, if you're into that sort of thing. Har har.

Some questions:

1.) *Collected Letters Vol. 2.* I'm having trouble finding a copy. Do you have any on hand? If so, how much? I live next door in Manitoba.

2.) Where did you buy your copies of *The Heart of Juliet Jones*? The only place I can find them is direct from the publisher at ClassicComicsPress.com

3.) I came late to the party in discovering Harvey Pekar and, like most, had no idea who he was until watching *American Splendor.* Most of his trade paperbacks line my bookshelf and, having a blue-collar background myself, am regularly experiencing a kinship with him through his stories. The autobio model, as also done so wonderfully by Eddie Campbell in *Alec,* is of great deal of interest to me. At least, the behind-the-scenes lives of creators. Whether creators only are the audience for such works, I don't know, but regardless, it's an appreciated genre in comics for this fanboy. Is autobio something you've considered? I guess *Cerebus Archive* would fall under that category, even *Glamourpuss* as it's your investigation in the Drake/Raymond relationship and car crash—actually, never mind, *Cerebus* is that, too. Okay, so how about maybe something with Dave Sim as the clear-cut subject matter? Which makes me wonder, has a autobio movie offer/proposal ever been presented to you?

November 23, 2012

Gee, can't believe I've waited this long to finish this letter, but truth be told, I had the C4 Comic Con early this month and September and October was spent writing, editing, producing and publishing two full novels for it, so they had to be my focus. Produced around 160,000 words between the two.

On a possible discussion note:

A hard lesson I've learned lately is the opposition by most to an objective point of view about things. Case in point: recently there was a dispute with some people regarding a Christmas gift exchange and, of course, gift cards came up. There is a $20-25 budget for these gifts and I pointed out that if we're all going to get each other gift cards, there was really no point in exchanging gifts. It's just equal dollars for equal dollars. How about a regular Christmas card and call it good? There was a lot of opposition to the comment, definitely feeling-driven, and it just amazed me that no one was willing to see the black-and-white of the issue save one person, possibly two. This also led to a discussion about what I might perceive as black-and-white isn't necessarily what another perceives as black-and-white, when in reality, objectivity isn't about perception (hence why it's called "objectivity"). Yet people still seem to think opinion factors into that. Sorry, no. Either something is or isn't, and that's it.

But I will admit it does create—at least right now—a sense of loneliness and even rejection. So much for telling it like it is. Maybe I'll just stick to "telling it like it is" in my novels and comics and blame the characters for my own shortcomings.

On a pretentious chit-chat note:

Winter's finally arrived here in Winnipeg. That north wind makes me glad I spend most of my time indoors.

Last:

Hope you're keeping well and congrats on the IDW deal for the *Cerebus* covers. You can write me down as a customer for that one as I often Google up the *Cerebus* covers and look at all 300 from time to time.

Hope to hear back from you.

Best,

Ps. This letter is my first out-going fax via this printer/scanner/fax thing I got. If there was a prize for it, it'd be yours, but I haven't found too many trophies with a golden guy standing by a fax machine receiving a piece of paper. I'll keep my eyes open, though. Har har. Bad joke. Close curtain. Try the veal and tip the waitress on your way out.

David Moody

December 4, 2012

Hi David,

How have you been? It's been a good while since we spoke. Like you, I've been cranking out the zombie fiction and just released the final book in my *Undead World Trilogy* called *Redemption of the Dead.* You had provided a blurb for the first one, *Blood of the Dead*, back in 2008. (Thanks again for that.)

I needed to get copies of *Redemption of the Dead* printed locally for a recent comic con and a printer here in Winnipeg came through on a VERY short deadline. I picked up the remainder of the books today and the manager of operations, Rene, asked me if I knew you. I said yes. Turns out he picked up a copy of *Dogblood* the other day and since it reminded him of my stuff, he asked about the connection. As a thank you to him for his speedy service, I thought I'd get in touch with you and ask if you'd be willing to send him a quick note of (thanks or story links or something) as a surprise? I'm sure he'd be thrilled to hear from you. I didn't tell him I'd contact you. Wanted it to be a surprise. Is this cool? His email is ********@*******

Thanks for any help.

Hope you're keeping good and I'm still waiting for *Hater* to hit theatres. Is that still happening?

Peace.

Tim Webber
A Moment of Cerebus

Hi Tim,

Oh wow, I was just going to today mail Dave proof I signed his petition so I could hear back from him and this came in. Awesome. Yes, by all means, please run the points. To make it easy for you, I've copy/pasted them into this email.

If at all possible, can a "signature" be added for the sake of weblinks? ie.

A.P. Fuchs
Writer/Artist Axiom-man Comic Book Series
http://www.axiom-man.com

Feel free to drop me a note if you need anything further. I also enclosed an Axiom-man cover graphic should you wish to incorporate that into the article as well.

Happy New Year.

God bless. Please pass onto to Dave I hope he has a good New Year, too.

Thanks.

The eight points and precursors:

Here is my current model. I'm open to any feedback and/or suggestions and/or "what you're doing is crazy" comments.

Since my company is web-based, with 95% of books ordered being online (whether for print or eBooks), the remaining 5%

sold at conventions and booksignings, and since I've been able to sustain a living for close to three years based on that, and given the state of tech these days, I think I'm onto something.

Though I've slipped recently due to a major burn-out but am now getting back on track, I agree that, as you've stated—can't remember where—that when folks ask you for the secret to *Cerebus*'s success, you said keeping the book on time is the reason. I believe you. On-time books keep readers interested, give them their fix at regular intervals, and, assuming the sales are there, enables the creator to maintain a steady level of interest as he can sink all his time into his book instead of dividing the comic against a day job.

My model:

1.) Release the book on time in print, electronic download, and twice a week post a page from the comic on Mondays and Thursdays (see www.axiom-man.com). The reason for the webcomic is to raise awareness of the character to help feed print sales and downloads, likewise, if folks like what they read, they will be apt to pick up one or more of my novels.

2.) Forego Diamond for the print periodicals. Due to finances, discounts and such, I'm opting out of Diamond Distribution for the monthly book, instead releasing the copies of the comic for direct sale, short-running each issue at 300 copies. This cost enables me to keep the price low on the book and still make close to a buck an issue. Direct sales include direct ordering, conventions, booksignings, and trunk-of-the-car sales.

3.) Release each print issue through Ka-Blam.com (which is like Comix Press), and utilize their print and digital storefront at Indyplanet.com and Indyplanetdigital.com respectively.

4.) Release each issue in digital format through as many channels as possible (Kindle, Nook, iPad et al.), treating each download as if they are the print counterpart. A sale's a sale, after all.

5.) Once a particular story arc is complete, collected into a graphic novel. Also, ala Mike Mignola, include a bonus story to set the graphic novel apart from the periodical book.

6.) Use Diamond for graphic novel distribution.

7.) Use my printer's amazing distribution system to make the graphic novel available to all the online hotspots like Amazon.com and its sister sites, Barnes and Noble.com, and others. Also offer for direct sale, whether by order, conventions, booksignings, trunk-of-the-car sales, etc.

8.) Offer the graphic novel at a fair price for digital download via all the same channels the periodical was. Perhaps offer the same direct as long as I can ensure proper shopping cart procedure and security through services out there that specialize in online digital product ordering.

Part of being a one-man-band, as you know, is time management as it would be all too easy to turn the running of the company into the fulltime job and not the creating of comics. All of what I mentioned above—aside from direct sales—is based on the do-the-work-once-than-don't-worry-about-it model I've been using for eight years. This then frees up time for creating, marketing, and personal time with family. Might even be time for sleep, if you're into that sort of thing. Har har.

Later that afternoon:

Dear Tim:

Further to my previous note, in my excitement in sending you a reply, I only noticed my own att'd letter to Dave *instead* of Dave's reply, so that said, can you add this to the listing/article as Dave brought up an interesting point?

Regarding points 4 and 7, the "et al." and "etc.," these were written to save Dave reading through a list of distributors and thus giving him a dry letter. The truth is, points 4 and 7 are almost unending, point 7 more than 4, and I'd be happy to add to them on my *How to Self-publish Books and Comics the Right Way* blog at http://selfpublishinghub.wordpress.com in the New Year.

The idea(l), I think, is to cast as wide a net as possible distribution-wise without unintentionally getting yourself into a sea of paperwork and a big mess of places to keep track of, in turn losing yourself in the chaos and losing money and time as a result. Streamlining is so critical when it comes to being a one-man operation.

Okay, that's it. Thanks, Tim.

Best,

Steven OGorman

January 28, 2013

Dear Steven:

It's been two weeks since your note. Sorry for not getting back to you sooner. I've been busy playing catch-up on numerous projects and business obligations so had to put certain correspondence on hold.

Glad you liked *Axiom-man: City of Ruin*. I was really pleased with it myself and am thinking that for the next one, I'm going to do a "rush job" like I did for *City of Ruin*, that is, not rush the book just to get it done, but rather go all-out again in terms of writing a ton of words a day. I wrote that book very quickly, but the momentum seemed to come through in a positive way straight through to the big ending and the final reveal. I really love the ending as well and am particularly proud of it. I think it worked perfectly for the aim: for Valerie to learn Gabriel is Axiom-man. It's going to be exciting to see how this plays out in future books.

As said, I'm wrapping up a pile of things and this same wrapping up is why I couldn't get Episode Two out for Christmas. That's the next book, though. It's the last story that takes place before the comic. I have an idea of what I want to do, but as a clue, I want to do a story with next-to-no tights and capes. I'm thinking Gabriel will be either in his civies most of the time or in disguise as someone else. You'll see. Something different, but something that makes sense leading into the next full-lengther because, as per Oscar Owen's line in *City of Ruin*, he's got something big planned for Axiom-man and I've had this scheme of his ready for a few years. Just needed to wait for the right time to put it in the story.

I hope to have the next episode out before summer and the new full-lengther by C4 in November.

Not sure if you read my *Undead World Trilogy* yet, but the world in those books is the same world Axiom-man visited in *The Dead Land*.

Take Care.

Justin Shauf

February 4, 2013

Hey man,

Thanks for sending the PDF of *The Purple Bean.*

Honest opinion, nothing personal, of course:

The Good:

As mentioned in the next bit, I really liked the childlike voice to this. Reads authentic on a children's book front. Tell Abby I said she did an excellent job. Your art, as always, is bang on. Good job. I didn't analyze every line, but I can, if you want. (i.e. making sure people have the right amount of fingers, there's a stray black make on page 15, etc.). Donovan did an amazing job with the coloring, giving it more attention and detail than I expected. I thought it was going to be mostly flats with a few gradients here and there.

The behind-the-scenes idea is a good one—makes it unique as I haven't seen a children's book that does this—but see the notes below.

The Not as Good:

Why does it go from page 12 back to 10 then to 15 at the end? Also, as per the PDF, look closely as the pages seem to be different sizes. Check your source file.

Though you'll get different opinions on it, I think the last page on the top corner should have a comma, so, ". . . love it, too."

I fully understand your kid wrote it and it definitely carries that kind of "voice," but the ending was very abrupt. Personal opinion. Any chance on getting her to think of another page or two to wrap it up more neatly? Something about the person getting it then wanting to share it like the fairy did, maybe? This would also help balance it with the extensive guide at the end, which is 12 pages, which is the same length of the actual story itself.

The technical:

Get rid of the double spaces between sentences. Looks odd on the page.

Check a similar children's book you have and see if a gutter is need to compensate for the saddle stitch. I'm assuming the book should open fairly flat given its length (which you need to make to an even number of pages for the printer, not 29, an odd number). If you do add a gutter—and if you have one, you hid it well—the you'll have to stretch the art a bit, which can make things tricky. FYI, anyway.

Suggest darkening the purple outline for the cover test as--at least on my screen--it's too washed out; also remember, though, that as per my personal experience, whatever color you see on your screen ends being printed a shade/touch darker in hardcopy.

Same with the interior outline.

Behind-the-scenes page editing: The Purple Bean should be in italics. And "Presented here . . . are the entire PAGES not page."

Coloring thing at the end: second paragraph should be indented

95% sure it's "further from the truth," not farther given the individual words' definitions.

Want to send me the .psd of Donovan's thing? It needs an edit. Too many issues to list here.

Your bit has spelling issues, too. Want to send me the .psd?

The book looks great otherwise. Just needs a polish, which I realize can get tedious towards the end of the production side of things hence why getting a fresh pair of eyes on it really helps.

Let me know.

Sincerely,

Kristian Saint-Michel

Feb. 18, 2013

Dear Kristian Saint-Michel,

Thanks for the invitation to do your "25 Questions" for your blog. I accept. Feel free to send them to this email address and I'll fill them out as quickly as able.

Also glad to hear you enjoy the Axiom-man series. Do you read the books or the comics, or both? *City of Ruin*, the latest full-length book, came out a few months ago, in case you weren't aware.

Thanks again.

Sincerely,

Brian John Mitchell
QRD

February 25, 2013

Dear Brian,

Thanks for dropping me a line about doing an interview for your site. Just letting you know I got your email and am now finally able to respond. I will get these 25 questions back and answered to you as soon as possible.

Thanks again.

Sincerely,

Kristian Saint-Michel

March 10, 2013/March 18, 2013

Dear Kristian:

Sorry I was so long in getting these to you. I've been ill, first with a cold then with a touch of the flu and am finally recovering. Then so much work had to be done I can't see to finish anything these days.

Anyway, here are the 25 questions. I plan on saving a copy of this letter for my collected letters book and reprinting it there. Hope that's okay.

Here they are:

1. Who was the last person you told "I love you"?

My kid.

2. What will you find in your refrigerator if you looked right now?

Tons of vegetables as the Mrs. and I are doing a detox program called The Clean Program by Dr. Junger.

3. What was the last expletive that you used?

I try not to use those, but they slip now and then. Can't remember the word. A bad one?

4. When was the last time you cried?

With tears, maybe a month ago. Without tears, yesterday, in the shower. Remembered something I did once and tore me up inside.

5. What is the worst tasting thing you have ever eaten?

There's plenty, but roasted chestnuts are on my "never eat again" list.

6. In the film of your life, who plays you and what is the title?

Since most people say I look like him, I'll go with Jason Biggs. A fitting title would be *Onward,* as the pain and trials I've endured nearly killed me on more than one occasion, but I'm still standing. And by "killed me," I mean that literally, not as a metaphor.

7. What is the last furry thing that you touched?

My wife's ladybug pillow.

8. When was the last time you had a hangover?

Don't remember as I gave up getting drunk years ago. My brother came over for some PS3 the other week. I had one beer and an hour later I had a headache. Does that count?

9. Do you remember the last time you saw a random act of kindness?

Sadly, no. Wish that wasn't the case. Granted, I'm a homebody and don't leave the house very often.

10. If your iPod could only hold 3 songs, what would they be?

If I had an iPod, they'd probably be: *How Great Thou Art, The Last Recluse, American Splendor.*

11. What are you currently reading?

Clean by Dr. Alejandro Junger.

12. Have you ever broken someone's heart?

If you mean actual heartbreak where someone is genuinely affected by it and doesn't recover quickly? Unfortunately, yes. I regret it and swore I'd never break a heart again no matter what that might mean for me. Having been someone who has had their heart crushed by someone else, I could never intentionally visit that pain on another. It hurts far too much and, if it truly is a heartbreak by someone you love, it doesn't repair. Ever. I'd rather be miserable and them be happy then to let what happened to me happen to someone else, especially on my account. There's far too much pain in the world so if I could avoid visiting that on another and me pay the price, it's worth it.

13. If personalities had an odor, what would you smell like?

Cinnamon.

14. You are running in a race and overtake the second-place runner. What position are you now in?

The one before two . . .

15. Describe your happy place?

Dark room, small, a few blankets, a firm pillow and sheer peace and quiet. You know? The kind of silence that you can almost hear because it's so quiet and feels so good. Take me there, please.

16. What is the longest period that you have ever gone without taking a bath?

Months, perhaps even up to a year. But that's not taking a bath. You didn't say anything about breaks between showers.

17. What is your theme song?

Though I'm Canadian, "American Splendor" by Eytan Mirsky really resonates. Harvey Pekar and I have a lot in common and I'm saddened he's gone. Would love to have connected with him somehow, and in the close-knit world of pop culture, comics and books, he and I probably shared similar connections somewhere down the line.

18. Have you ever been spanked or spanked someone as an adult?

Growing up, yeah, quite a lot and I'm glad for it. They call it "hitting a child" nowadays, but we also live in a world where people don't understand the meaning of half of the words they speak and hitting a kid versus spanking them are two different things with two different motives.

19. What do you do when you feel sad or depressed?

Sleep. I get very tired and quickly shutdown.

20. If you were being attacked by the tickle monster, who would you want it to be?

I don't do tickles.

21. Do you believe in ghosts? Why?

Certainly, but not in the dead people sense. As a Christian and having had brushes with the supernatural on both sides of the coin, demons sometimes use the guise of ghosts to interact with people. My wife has had supernatural encounters you wouldn't believe, but that was before she was saved. It's been fine since.

22. Describe the perfect kiss using no more than 5 words?

Soft, deep, meaningful.

23. What is your greatest fear?

Standing before God on Judgment Day and not making the cut.

24. What is the best dish you can cook?

I do a pretty good shrimp gumbo.

25. Do you truly feel loved?

Honestly? No, but that's something I've always struggled as far back as I can remember. I've been through so much pain that it's hard to think someone actually cares about me—genuinely cares—despite what they might say. That's being straight up on the subject.

There you go, Kristian. Thanks for the questions. Please let me know when you run it so I can help spread the word.

Sincerely,

Brian John Mitchell
QRD

March 18, 2013

Dear Brian:

I know it's been a long time coming, but here is that interview I promised you. Thanks so much for conducting it.

Name: A.P. Fuchs
City: Winnipeg
Comics: Axiom-man, Canister X
Websites: http://www.canisterx.com, http://www.axiom-man.com, http://www.coscomentertainment.com, http://www.tornveilbooks.com

1. How old were you when you first got into comics & did you always stick with them or did you come back to them?

As a reader, I read them here and there growing up, but it wasn't until I was about fifteen that I got into them both to read and to want a career in. I drew all the time in high school, took a year off afterward, then went to animation school. When that school stopped teaching its curriculum half way through the year, I got soured toward the whole art community and switched to writing comics and books. I launched my company, Coscom Entertainment, in 2004 and published a couple of graphic novels through the imprint—not my own material—and one Axiom-man comic written by me and drawn by another. It wasn't until 2007 that I started seriously thinking about getting into comics again in terms of putting out stuff written and drawn by myself and, finally, 2011 is when I started publishing comics more regularly. I'm still not publishing as often as I would like though and plan on rectifying that this year. The price I pay for being a novelist and running two publishing imprints at the same time. Really regret abandoning it for a while, however. Real dumb move.

2. What was the first comic book you ever bought?

My mom bought me a *Quasar* issue when I was a kid. I don't have it anymore, but I still remember certain parts. In terms of my own money, I might have gotten something when I was young, but I do know that when I started collecting when I was fifteen it was *Nightwing* #1 and DC's *The Final Night* #1.

3. How old were you when you put out your first comic?

Twenty-seven for *Axiom-man: Of Magic and Men*, but I didn't draw that one. I was thirty when *Canister X* No. 1 came out. I did produce a full comic back in my high school drawing days, but it was never published. Still have it somewhere.

4. What decade do you think produced the best comics?

I'd say the '90s *solely* because there was the black-and-white boom and the Image boom. Sure, not all of it was great—I mean, the stories were backseat with the art being the big deal at the time—but some good stuff came out of it (Jeff Smith, Terry Moore, etc.). Further, it was cool that people published pretty much anything, which meant the reader could decide what they liked even if not everyone agreed. Sort of a readers buffet, something that doesn't exist anymore.

5. Why comics instead of just writing or drawing?

That's the thing, though: I do both, that is, I'm also a novelist. But for me, comics hold a special place since I've always been a superhero fan and superheroes originated in the comic world, at least the ones that we know nowadays. Comics is a medium where anything can happen, and because you're also playing with visuals aside from narrative, you can achieve layers of storytelling you can't get in novels alone. Readers can take in comics quickly, slowly, mix it up—anyway they want, really, and how they take it in changes how they experience the story. A friend of mine reads the comics then goes back and just looks at the art. He gets the story two ways that way. Reading books—you can read slowly, but it's all very linear and very paced out as a result, therefore limiting even your imagination. Same with movies where you're told what to see, when to see it, when to hear it, what mood to feel thanks to the music—With comics, each panel is a window into a different world and you can hang around there as long as you want without being prompted to get out and move to the next panel unless you let yourself.

6. Do you see mini-comics & indie comics as paths to mainstream comics or as their own unique media?

Minis or indie comics and mainstream are all the same in that they're comics. The issue is audience size, but even then that can be argued because, for example, when *Cerebus*, an indie publication, was at its peak, Dave Sim had some 30,000 monthly readers, certainly a number high enough to be considered mainstream. I'm not really a fan of the divide between the "indie world" and the "mainstream world." There are parties on both sides that strive to keep the walls up between the two, but in reality it's all comics. Does volume of readers really matter? Why is that a measuring point?

Yes, indie comics and/or mini comics can be bridge to the mainstream. I've already mentioned their names, but will do so again: Jeff Smith and Terry Moore. Jeff still self-publishes but he also has taken *Bone* mainstream with Scholastic. Terry does work-for-hire for Marvel now and then while still doing his own thing via his Abstract Studio imprint.

7. How many copies of your comic do you print in your first run?

For *Axiom-man: Of Magic and Men*, I think it was 50. *Canister X* No. 1 was 100. *Axiom-man* No. 1 was 300, I think.

8. How much do you think comics should cost?

Depends on page count, but for 20 pgs black and white, a couple bucks (though no one charges this). For full color, $3 tops. Unfortunately, printing costs don't allow for this unless your print run is super high so we're stuck with $3 or so for black and white and $4-plus for color. It's too bad. I understand how time-consuming comics are to make, I really do. Just wish there was a better way, but unfortunately there's not. Not yet, anyway. However, the digital market makes it easier to lower the price because aside from the artist's time creating the book, there's no overhead printing-wise.

9. How many books do you produce a year & how many would you like to?

Right now two or three. That's comics, so not including my novels, which varies from two to four on top of that. I'd like to do a monthly comic, or at least six forty-page issues of *Axiom-man* and six twenty-to-twenty-four-page issues of *Canister X* a year. Trying to free up my schedule so I can do that.

10. Do you think stories should be serialized or delivered as complete works?

It depends. For the sake of market presence you need serialization, doing it monthly or, say, every six weeks. If creators could get two or three graphic novels out a year, then that would be okay, too, but they'd have to stay in front of readers' faces between books via marketing efforts. And doing two or three graphic novels a year isn't farfetched either. I mean, a page a day. If you're graphic novels are 100-120 pages, you can do three no problem. You just need the work ethic and treat it as a job even if it's not your main source of income. What you put in is what you get out, you know?

11. How are comic strips different than comic books & which medium do you prefer?

Strips are shorter, usually with a punchline after three or four panels. Comic books are longer stories with more panel variation presentation-wise. I prefer comic books as I can get more into them than just strips. Then there's graphic novels, which goes beyond just collecting a bunch of comic books and calling it one. Graphic novels as a medium is the epitome, to me.

12. How long is it from when you start a comic until it's printed?

When I decided it's time for a new issue and work properly—and it's not a 24-hour comic—then about a month.

13. What do you do better with your comics now than when you first started?

Putting more detail into the panels and sticking to my own voice.

14. Do you do thumbnails?

Sort of. I write my scripts as terribly-drawn comic panels with stick figures in notebooks. That way I can write my story at around the same pace I do a novel. When I go back to draw the comic for real, I understand my own gibberish and crude panels so know what I meant and finish fleshing it out on the drawing board.

15. At what size do you draw?

For *Canister X*, 8.5" x 11" as the final print size is digest size. For *Axiom-man*, it's on 11" x 17" Bristol board with a 10" x 15" live area.

16. What kind of pens do you use?

All kinds. Sharpies, bics (no, really), fat permanent markers, micron, marvy 1122 le plume 2, some sort of roller grip pen. Whatever works, really.

17. What does your workstation look like?

A mess. Well, not really. It's your basic drawing board with my page taped onto it, a lamp hanging over it, and a lettering chart I made that shows the size I need to letter at in order for it to be the right size once reduced and printed. I also tape on my notebook open to the sketch page so I know what I'm drawing. It keeps falling down but since I'm such a archive/collector kind of guy, I'm too chicken to rip the pages out and tape those down instead. On the side of the drawing desk are some shelves with notebooks and odds and ends. Nothing fancy.

18. At what point in the artistic process do you work digitally?

Scanning. Put it into the computer and then clean up all the stray bits that wound up on the page from either erasing, my dirty fingers, mistakes that were whited out then inked over, smears, etc.

19. What do you think of digital comics & webcomics?

Axiom-man is a webcomic and I'm using it as an entry point for readers/a means of advertising a character not everyone has heard of. No risk to the reader that way. The comic isn't solely web, though, as I do publish digital and print versions of *Axiom-man* as well. Same with *Canister X*, though for that one I don't do a webcomic. I do post the occasional short story from it, though, over at my blog.

Digital comics, that is, monthly comics but just digital, I think, will replace the normal floppies as the serial version of the work, but ultimately print graphic novels will be king.

20. Do you prefer working in color or black & white?

Black and white. Without sounding pretentious, there's something organic and honest about it. It also forces you to show your best work because you can't hide your lines or mistakes with a bunch of flashy gradients or color effects. Some would argue the coloring is part of the art, too, but in the age of digital coloring, it's easy to mask your work with effects.

21. How many different people should work on a comic & what should their jobs be?

Don't think there's a set amount. In the mainstream, it takes seven people or more—see the credits page of any DC comic—which is also why I think corporate comics are in such dire straits right now. In the end, isn't one person all you need, someone who treats each page as a piece of art and does all the tasks involved in creating it?

22. How do you find collaborators?

I used to post on Digital Webbing years and years ago, but now it's just me so I collaborate with myself. I don't have to go far to find me if I need me. Usually.

23. How tight do you think a script should be as far as telling the artist what to draw?

Depends on whose vision the comic is, which is something I think the artist and writer need to work out ahead of time. Once decided, then the final script would reflect that even if they decide the book will be a true fifty-fifty split.

24. What comic book person would you be most flattered to be compared to?

Dave Sim or Alan Moore.

25. What do your friends & family think of your comics?

This is a loaded question, actually, so I'll summarize it by simply saying that back when I started it was in the "Oh, that's nice," category. Nowadays, I know I'm supported in terms of using my art as a career, but I really don't know what they think of my work. They've bought some of it, but there isn't much feedback.

My wife and kids think it's cool, though. The kids have already started drawing their own comics and stapling them together in books.

26. What do you think of superheroes?

Love them. Lifelong fan. In fact, every single story I tell is somehow a superhero story, even the novels I've written that don't blatantly have guys in tights. I'm practically obsessed with them.

27. Marvel or DC?

DC.

28. What comic characters other than your own would you like to work with?

Superman or Batman, I think.

29. Ideally would you self-publish?

Already am. The idea of working for a mainstream house doesn't appeal to me as I'm not a fan of corporations, and after hearing the horror stories that have recently made the news about comic creators leaving certain major companies—yeah, I'm fine with where I'm at. I wouldn't turn down a gig if it was offered to me, but it's not an aspiration of mine. I'm happy just doing my own thing.

30. What conventions do you try to attend & why?

Central Canada Comic Con (www.c4con.com). It's local, it's pretty big, and I do well there sales-wise as I got a lot of support from my hometown. That's a priority show for me. They also have a smaller show, which I'll be doing in a couple weeks as well. I would love to attend APE or SPX, however. One day, hopefully sooner rather than later.

31. What do you do to promote your books?

Everything from website stuff like blogging, to social networks like Facebook and Twitter, to conventions, book signings, trunk-of-car sales, interviews, giving away free books, promo cards, fliers . . .

32. Do you think your comics are well suited to comic shops or would sell better elsewhere?

Do comic shops still sell comics? Seems they're over half toys and card games now. Okay, bad joke, but I think *Axiom-man* would work just fine in a mainstream shop. *Canister X* would have to be in a zine and/or minicomics section. Sadly, most of the mainstream comic readership doesn't know what a minicomic or zine is. It'd be great if all comic shops had an indie rack for those kinds of publications.

33. What other medium would you like to see some of your comics made into (television, film, games, action figures, etc.)?

Film, definitely. There's an indie filmmaker I know who's been bugging me to lend him my Axiom-man costume so he can film a book trailer for *The Axiom-man Saga.* I'd really like to see a live action movie with Axiom-man though, whether something for the mainstream or even just for the direct market.

I'm also hoping someone will knock on my door and do a documentary about me, that is, my work and what it's like to be a fulltime writer and artist, the ups and downs, the work schedule, etc.

34. Do you consider yourself a comic collector or a comic reader or both?

Definitately both, same with books, which is why I don't have an eReader. If I just read and that was it, I'd have one in a heartbeat. But I need actual books and comics because I love being surrounded by them. Having long boxes lying around, graphic novels on the shelves—love it.

35. What do you see as the most viable mediums for comics distribution 10 years from now?

Only one: the Internet. How a person accesses it ten years from now remains to be seen, but digital comics and print-on-demand paperbacks will be the norm, I think. If anything, print comics will be more "special edition" and digital comics will be the mass market. Same with books.

36. What would you like to see more people doing with comics?

Making more of an effort to get their books out there, namely independent cartoonists. Most just want to draw, but the reality is you need to spend half your time drawing, the other half doing business stuff. Even more than half your time doing business stuff. That's talking from experience and that's if you want to succeed. Sounds arrogant and I don't mean it that way, but coming from the school of hard knocks, I know what I'm talking about. Your audience won't come to you. You need to find them, show them your stuff, and keep them.

37. Anything else?

Please, everyone, support indie comic creators and indie book writers. If you read something of theirs, write a review on Amazon, like their product so it shows up on your Facebook page, tweet about them and help spread the word. The issue isn't about the money—though that helps the artist to keep producing in a timely manner—but your support goes a long way in spreading the word about the independent publishing world and the titles available. Most of us are one-man bands. We can't do it alone and compete with the marketing machines of big corporations who tell you what to buy. Thanks in advance if you step up.

Thanks for the interview, Brian. This was fun. Please be sure to let me know when you run it so I can help spread the word.

I've attached a plethora of images for you to choose from, formatted to your specs. Feel free to run however many of them you wish. One is for the header, the others for the sidebar.

RSVP if you need anything further. God bless.

Sincerely,

Kristian Saint-Michel

April 11, 2013

Hi,

Looks good except for this one small bit:

"Fuchs also writes non-fiction, Twitters a lot and writes in his blog–that's here–5 to 6 days a week, sometimes more than once a day. His Twitter address is http://www.twitter.com/ap_fuchs, so be sure to follow as it's always fun."

The line "that's here" is from my website where I blog versus yours where this is posting, so I suggest removing that.

Down the list where you ask who could play me in a movie, "Jason Biggs" should be two words not one.

Otherwise, yes, looks good to me. Run with it. Let me know when it's up and I'll spread the word.

Thanks again for interviewing me.

Sincerely,

Rhiannon Paille
C4 Lit Fest

April 11, 2013

Hi,

Here are my thoughts on the stories submitted for the C4 Lit Fest Short Story contest. My top three are listed at the end. Wrote a couple of sentences for each story in terms of feedback.

Aokigahara by Colin Enquist – It's okay. At first I wasn't too interested, but then I saw where it was going. Short stories written in first person are easier to write than third person so for a contest, I have to dock it points for that. *6 out 10*

End of the Line by J.D. Hay - Stopped reading after the first couple pages. Formatting is completely wrong. I don't know if you had guidelines, but general story formatting should be learned by every writer.

Gilly: gaijin/Galician/ghost owl by Ariel Gordon - Formatting. A story should never be submitted in Arial. Garamond or Times, please. No proper indenting or paragraph formatting. To me, basics like this should be known. Seems superficial, but at the same time, if a writer wants me to take them seriously, I expect them to know how the biz works in terms of proper submission. Using ampersands instead of "and" is lazy. Stopped reading after the first page. Writing needs work, too.

Goodbye Kid by Katrine Deniset - Punctuation and formatting issues. Also in first person, which bothers me in terms of showcasing writing skill. Not that first person is a sin, but it's a much easier way to write and not a good way to show off skills.

Stopped reading after the first page and a half. Too many spelling issues as well.

Stick-up or Pick-up by Andreas Oertel - Another first person story. Pet peeve of mine for the aforementioned reason. Easily the best formatted and presented thus far. Good use of build-up tension as we waited for the robbery to occur. Like the positive twist at the end. *7.5 out of 10*

Ruth's Story by it doesn't say - Stopped reading after first paragraph, skimmed the rest. Language much too flowery and pretentious. Writing needs a lot of work. Major punctuation issues. Sorry.

Some Days Seem to Last Forever by Judy Stoddart - First person. Suggest making third person mandatory for next year. Just my opinion, though. Same with some formatting guidelines as this one was hard to read. I kept going because the writing was the best I've read today thus far. Reads like a sincere blog entry on a mommy blog. Hard to rate because the story wasn't really about anything, but writing-wise it was good, so I'll tie it with *Stick-up or Pick-up* for *7.5 out of 10.*

The Burden by Jennifer Kushnier - First person again. Lots of punctuation trouble and some spelling issues. It did a good job on creating a sense of intrigue, however. *6.5 out of 10*

The Ghost in the Coffee Shop by Nicky Dandurand - Another first person story. Due to improper paragraph formatting, I stopped reading after the first couple paragraphs (which were really supposed to be broken up into three for four, easily). Really messes with the story.

The Haggard Man by Melinda Friesen - First person. This writer took a chance by writing in the present tense, which is tricky. Overall, Melinda did a good job. Some punctuation trouble. Out of all the stories, this one is the most exciting so far, and not because it's horror. The ending wasn't finite enough for me, or finite-with-an-open-ending enough either, so it lost points for that.7.5 for sure, leaning towards an *8 out of 10.*

The Master Cell by George Nicholas Alexander Cornier - I'm sorry, but I'm not sure how to read this so I passed after the first few paragraphs. The paragraphs, misspelled words, the different colors—at first I thought maybe it was supposed to be a series of text messages or something. I just don't know.

Toothpicks by Myles S. Hildebrand - First person. Writing's not bad. Started strong, but seemed to falter toward the end. Good piece of flash fiction, though. Had a clear beginning, middle and end so I was satisfied that way. A clear sign of someone who understands writing structure. *7 out of 10.* If only the writing didn't slip as the story went on.

Uploaded by Russell Dew - Stopped reading on the second page. The story seemed interesting, but it was all telling and no showing, plus improper paragraph structure.

So, as per this list here, it looks like *Stick-up or Pick-up*, *Some Days Last Forever* and *The Haggard Man* are the top three, the last being the best one. I'd even through *Toothpicks* in because of the beginning, middle and end aspect of it, but *The Haggard Man* is top dog for me.

Thanks for letting me put my two cents in as a judge. Was fun to read stories I didn't have any potential publishing interest in. I mean that in a good way.

I realize you're not offering writers critique opportunities at the Lit Fest. Can I do this independently? Have a small sign at my table or whatever? I'll give you 10% as a finder's fee. Please let me know either way. After reading these stories, I'm motivated to do so since, a long time ago, I had someone run my stuff through the wringer and I learned a whole ton. If I can extend it to others, I'd be happy to do so.

RSVP

Thanks.

Sincerely,

Rhiannon Paille
C4 Lit Fest

April 12, 2013

Hi,

Here is my comments on the late entry: *Snow Globe* by Connie McDonald/Reevie.

A third person story. Big deal for me. She even formatted it properly as Courier, 12pt, double-spaced—standard manuscript formatting. This goes a long way presentation-wise. The writing needs a lot of work, however. Lots of punctuation issues and switching between tenses, point-of-view shifting, and just general beginner mistakes. In terms of the story, it's one of the most creative compared to the others and I was interested the whole time. The ending doesn't make sense though I get what the author was trying to do. *6 out of 10* for me, with a bonus point for proper submission formatting, so *7*.

The Haggard Man is still the winner for me.

Sincerely,

Jeffrey Allen Davis

April 14, 2013

Hi Jeff,

Oh wow, what an honor. Truly. I'd be thrilled to check out your book, *Invasion of the Ninja*, review it and, if I remember, put the opening of the box/enevlope on camera. (I keep meaning to do more Canister X Mailboxes, but I honestly just keep forgetting and open stuff before filming. I'm probably one of the few people who actually gets excited for the mailman to come as I get paid via the mail plus am currently in the process of trading zines and minicomics over the mail so have stuff coming in regularly) Thanks so much. Please autograph it for me. Is it available online yet? I'll give you a promo blurb on Facebook and Twitter to help spread the word.

I'm a ninja fan so this is very cool. Have you seen the Scott Adkins movie, *Ninja*? A sequel is due out this year last I heard. Likewise, *Ninja Assassin* was pretty sweet.

Please send your book to:

A.P. Fuchs
****
Winnipeg, MB
****
Canada

Please check off "gift" on the customs form so I don't accidentally get dinged a customs charge. Post office seems to be random in this regard, but doesn't hurt to be safe rather than sorry.

Thanks for thinking of me. To know that the first *Axiom-man* novel inspired you to self-publish means a great deal to me as it was Frank Dirscherl's original self-published *The Wraith* novel—along with *Knightseeker* by Eric Cooper—that inspired *me* to put Axiom-man out as a book. Originally, back in high school, Axiom-man was going to headline Coscom when Coscom was going to be a comic book company (inspired by Image Comics as in everything being creator-owned). Life's curveballs changed the plan and it wasn't until Frank's book did I learn you can self-publish your own superhero fiction. Call me naïve. This was back in 2004, I believe, when I first found Frank's book. Coscom Entertainment put out a hardback of it in 2005 with a paperback following shortly after. In January of 2006 was when I finally sat down to write *Axiom-man* despite having his story in my head for over a decade by that point.

The rest, as they say, is history though with my publishing duties, I haven't been able to write as many *Axiom-man* books as I would like to—I mean, there was four years between *The Dead Land* and *City of Ruin*, which is ridiculously way too long—so, between you , me and the lamppost, I'm in the process of pulling back from traditional publishing so I can focus on my own stuff as the *Axiom-man Saga* is set to be 25 novels, 25 novellas, and however many short stories and comics until it's complete. So far, I only have 3 novels and 2 novellas done aside from a few short stories and comics. Long ways to go so once things lighten up for me—hopefully starting in the summer—I'm going to be cranking this stuff out big time. To do 2 novels and 2 novellas a year plus comics would be the bee knees.

Anyway, how does that saying go? "Enough about me let's talk about me?" Haha. Kidding. But seriously, enough about my stuff. I'm excited to see your book. Let me know if there's a link so I can talk about it.

Thanks.

Rhiannon Paille
C4 Lit Fest

April 15, 2013

Hi,

Just when you thought you were out, they puuulll you back in. Kidding.

Here is my two cents on the late entries to the short story contest. Or is it "*are* my two cents" because there is more than one cent being added? I don't know. I blame all the tea I've been drinking thanks to this stupid cold.

Anyway:

Du Chat: My life as a Cat by Who-knows-who. Seriously. People need to start putting in bylines. Or is "Du Chat" the pen name and it was positioned wrong on the page? I don't know. This is first person. Stopped after a few a paragraphs. Spelling issues and enough grammar problems that I have to pass.

Hunted by Tori Holmberg. First person. As mentioned, you should say first person stories are allowed, but third person are preferred or something. In terms of what it was about, it was okay. There were a lot of elements that didn't make sense, however, and an explanation of the use of magic or what type of world we were in was completely absent. You can't just assume the reader knows what you're talking about in fiction. You need explain your world and rules. Just not in overkill, of course. There is *implied* explanation, but that's another topic. *5 out of 10.*

Redeemed or Validated by Who-knows-who. No byline loses points with me. Though not story-specific, simple writing presentation and formatting goes a looong way with editors. At least, for this one, it does. First person. This is the sign of a newbie writer, which is fine, but usually new writers or inexperienced ones write first person because it's easier. I know I did. Overuse of brackets was distracting, but this was one of the better-written ones over all. Just no ending. Hard choices. *7 out of 10*, factoring in no byline and bracket overusage.

Spirits of the North by Fasial Islam. First person. Easily in the top two writing-wise thus far. The ending—that's the secret. You need an ending and this story had one. Aside from bad paragraph presentation and font choice—Arial—this was good stuff. How particular should I be? I mean, this passes *The Haggard Man*, for me, but the presentation has issues. *8 out of 10* because of that and my first person pet peeve, but I think it's better written than *The Haggard Man.*

Fragment from The Lost Lovecraftian Ur-Text that Absolutely, Definitely did not come from Africa. Discovered and translated from Ur-language by Gabriel Wendt. Unique start with the title alone. That's good. This is a story that is about something yet nothing at all, clear and vague at the same time. Had this been a children's story, it would completely work, but otherwise, no, *5 out of 10.*

Prophecy Protection Squad by Who-knows-who. Creativity-wise, this one stands out, and I like how, unlike the other story, the magic used didn't seem like it came out of left field, but unfortunately, the writing quality and formatting issues hurt it quite a lot. *4 out of 10.*

The First Masterpiece by Carmela Co. Formatting issues and first person aside, it was well written. "I have to objectify my subject. I have to subjectify my object" ar probably the best lines in all of the short stories submitted for this contest. On the flip side, there is some overly-complicated language in here that, for me, I didn't know what was going on. In terms of emotion, this story has it, but it's not really about anything, that is, a beginning, middle and end. *7 out of 10.*

Warrior of the Night by Who-knows-who. There's good first person and there's bad first person. This was good first person. You can sense the emotion in this, and the writing, aside from a handful of slips, was top notch. To be honest, I think this is my new winner. It took a moment to figure out it was about a cat. I thought maybe a werewolf at first. Despite being a dog person, this one gets top placement. 9 out of 10, losing .5 for technical stuff, so *8.5 out of 10.*

Yametuk and the Golden Swirl by Rachel Hawryluk. Third person. Formatting issues and POV trouble, but overall the writing was pretty good actually. I like slice-of-life fiction when done right and using the kids as the main characters was done well. There was no ending, though, that is, it was tapering off as it should and then stopped short. Hard to judge. *7.5 out of 10.*

My choices have changed as a result, my top three being, in order:

Warrior of the Night
Spirits of the North
The Haggard Man

All right, time to start prepping my workshops because it'd be embarrassing to just stand there and ramble and not really "teach" per se.

Not sure if anyone is videotaping these workshops, but it would make great Youtube promo for all writers involved. Just an idea. I have a digital camera that does video, but not super great ones (see www.youtube.com/canisterx for the quality), but maybe I can swing picking up a new, cheap handheld my wife can handle and we can do some con highlights or something.

Sincerely,

Graeme Brown

May 2, 2013

Graeme,

Please forgive the disgustingly late reply. It's tax season for me and between crunching numbers and editing anthologies never mind all the other stuff that goes with running a publishing company, I've been so busy that "extra" correspondence has fallen by the wayside.

It was nice meeting you, too.

Congrats on the agreement with Champagne Books. I don't know a whole lot about them, but I'm glad you found folks to work with.

Self-publishing—despite the hype these days—is not something to take lightly, and is very much for the type of person who is hands-on and entrepreneurial by nature. Just uploading to Kindle isn't self-publishing. You really do need to run it as a business and, therefore, work at it as such. Gone are the days of writers only writing and that's it.

Your Thursday in the Spotlight feature on your blog sounds like it'd be fun. My door's open anytime for interviews so just fire me a note and we can get started.

Hope you can make it out to C4 in November. This year will be my seventh year tabling at it. It's always a blast and a special weekend for me. If you do come out, be sure to stop by and say hello.

Speaking of weekends, have a good one.

Sincerely,

Cynthia Holowachuk

June 5, 2013

Dear Cynthia,

It was nice meeting you, too, at the Litfest. I hope they do another one next year as this one seemed to be quite a success.

As per your questions, copy/pasted from your email:

1.) for first timer noveliest, would it be better to self publish or get a publisher and what are the riskes of both.

This is a loaded question. In the end, the best choice for the writer—first-timer or otherwise—is to decide what kind of career they're striving for and, no, being "rich and famous" isn't a career choice. Though it can happen in this business, it's not the norm nor should be anyone's pursuit. The thing with the traditional market or the independent one is that success largely depends on the author and how much effort he or she is willing to put into the book right from the writing of it, through the publication process and then upon release.

If the writer just wants to write, then try and find a traditional publishing house—small press, medium or big. However, if the writer just wants to write, I don't recommend even attempting a career in this business but instead would tell them to just write their stories for their own amusement on rainy days and call it good.

If the writer actually wants a career in publishing, they need to ask themselves if they're the business-running type of person or not. If they're entrepreneurial by nature, then self-publishing would be fun because to truly self-publish properly, it's about 80% business, 20% creative. You spend a lot of your time running your business, producing the books, marketing them, networking, footing the bill for art, editing, printing, etc., and growing the business. Just uploading your book to Kindle or something isn't self-publishing. I go into greater detail about this in my book, *Getting Down and Digital: How to Self-publish*, which is coming out late June.

If one isn't business-inclined, then working with a publisher is a better choice as the publisher handles the business end and the writer can then just work on writing the next book and spreading the word about their current releases.

For first-timers, doing their research about a publisher is critical and I would strongly suggest that if they do get offered a contract, to not sign on the dotted line simply because they got a contract and want to see their book in print. The last thing you'd want is to sign an agreement which you will later regret. Google the publishing house you're considering signing with it. Be specific and type in questions about people possibly having bad experiences with them.

And learn your craft. Just because you wrote a story or book doesn't mean it should be published. While true there are tons and tons of good stories out there, many of them are not written well, so while they might be good in terms of "what they're about," the presentation (the writing) isn't. Simply stringing a bunch of words together does not a writer make.

How you do write well? Like Stephen King says: write a lot and read a lot. Pay attention to what you're reading in terms of how the sentences are constructed. Look at the dialogue, the pacing, the action, how to format thoughts, proper point-of-view usage, those sorts of things. I get submissions all the time and most of the time the writer sending them in hasn't learned how to write properly. Also, in this day and age with all the self-publishing hype, books are published because people can publish more easily now more than ever, but what they're publishing shouldn't have come to market in the first place because they're poorly written.

2) Should the writer concider trends or niches to catter their writing to or should they just go ahead and start writing whatever they want. Are their any writing trends in winnipeg.

I've always recommended a writer write what they enjoy. To write only "what makes money" is—and I'm going to sound like a pretentious-artist—not a good display of artistic integrity. The thing is, too, that a reader can tell if the author is enthusiastic about what they're writing. It comes through on the page and if one is just going to be a hack and churn out something for a buck.

I mean, sure, you can pick a market and write for it, maybe even pay some or all of your bills with it, but will you enjoy it and turn out your best material? Probably not.

A better bet is to write that which you enjoy and find a market for that kind of work and build your audience that way. I mean, if you like something, odds are there are quite a few others out there who like what you like.

3) What are the best publishing houses in Winnipeg (cost, and safty)

To be honest, I'm not involved in Winnipeg's art scene. Used to be, but found it incredibly pretentious and stuffy so withdrew and now spend my time in the world of the underground and small press, whether that's with people elsewhere in Winnipeg or Canada, the States, UK, wherever.

4) How do they go about protecting them selfs from copy right protection

You mean copyright infringement? Once you write something, it's a done deal and is copywritten. You can add the "© copyright so-and-so 2013, all rights reserved" notice if you want to, or do the lazy man's copyright protection "insurance"—and I use the term loosely—by mailing a copy of your manuscript to yourself via registered mail. You can even officially register your copyright with the intellectual property office, too. Those last two are fail safes in case something legal comes up and you can't prove you wrote the book before the other guy or that the idea was originally yours.

In the end, something's copywritten once you write it so no official protection is technically needed. Really depends on how paranoid you are. But if you do write something and you know it's going to sit in a drawer for a long, long, long time, then consider some sort of registration.

5) what should they do to protect their material from anytheift or any other liability

Not sure what you mean. See above about the theft part. In terms of liability, that's a very broad term so if you think you're writing something where you could be liable for damages or a person or property, then talk to an attorney about how to protect yourself.

6) How can writers market them selves to reach their taget markest

Set up a website or blog, connect online *and* in person with like-minded people—in short find out where your market is and then simply meet them there.

If you're a fan of something, go to where those fans are. There's no real secret place where people are sitting around waiting to gobble up whatever you're creating.

7) How much does it cost to publish a novel

$0 - $1,000,000 or more. Really depends on what you're doing, what you can get for free, who you're dealing with, how you're dealing with them, the printing, the marketing, business costs, and loads more.

It's hard to give an average, but to do it *right*, most books cost $250 - $1000 at least, if not more.

I hope the above was helpful. They're big questions and I gave you the *Reader's Digest* answers, but they should be enough of a stepping stone(s) for whoever might be considering them.

You did right to ask these questions, though, because like I said, writers need to research potential publishers, markets, self-publishing and anything else to do with this every-changing business if they hope to navigate their way through it and have some semblance of a career making stuff up for a living.

They also need to consider find out if what they've written is even saleable because no writer turns out gold all the time.

Sincerely,

Ray Luczak

July 12, 2013

Dear Ray,

Thank you for email of June 10, 2011. Only now, a little over two years later, did I read it. The problem was the email address you sent it to—no fault of your own—as it was one I haven't checked in an incredibly long time for numerous reasons. For the past couple of weeks I've been going through and deleting the 13,000+ messages that have accumulated in there thus bringing us to today.

Your email letter telling me how much you enjoyed *April* really meant a lot. Thank you. I'm glad the book was able to have the impact that it did. It's an intensely personal book for me and so far is the only full length book I've released as Peter Fox. I have a novella written under that name which I plan on putting out sometime if I can ever get the book off disk and onto my computer as computers nowadays don't support 3.5" disks and my old computer which did is deceased.

The only other thing I've done as Peter Fox is a short story called "My Angel and Me," which is available on Kindle and other eBook sites. I did revisit the Joseph and April characters in my zombie trilogy, *Undead World*—written as myself—but, of course, that trilogy—while loaded with romantic themes—aren't the love story that *April* is.

As to your question if you can send me a copy of the book for signature, I'm open to that. Where are you located because if not in Canada then the whole enclosing return postage thing won't work? We'd have to deal with postage coupons or simply enclosing a chunk of change with book itself. The Paypal option you proposed for a signed copy would be easier, but at the same time, if you already have the book then I'd hate to force upon you a second. If you don't have it, then, yes, you can get a signed copy from me direct and the Paypal method would be best. Please let me know if you want it signed "Peter Fox" or "A.P. Fuchs" as I'm fine with either. Also let me know if you want it made out to you or not.

Hope this email finds you well. So terribly sorry for the late reply. You can reply to this email, however, as I'm checking this address regularly now.

Again, I'm really glad you liked the book and that you could relate to what was going on. Brings comfort to know I'm not theonly one who sometimes wonders "What if . . . ?"

Thanks.

Best,

Dave Sim

July 16, 2013

Dear Dave:

Well, back in March I found you sent me a copy of *Collected Letters Vol. 2* complete with a Cerebus head sketch and signature as you promised in your previous letter to me. You took me by surprise. Not that I didn't think you'd send it, but rather, as per the letter, it was to be part of our book swap and I expected I'd send my part first then you'd send yours after. Thanks for going out of your way to send the book before you got mine.

I'm about halfway through reading it and am enjoying it as much as the first one. I noticed the change in format: smaller trim, less pages. If I recall, in a previous letter you sent me waaaaay back in 2007 (I think), you said you had enough letter material to fill some fifteen volumes of *Collected Letters*. Why did you not opt for a phone book for this one? Just a publisher-to-publisher curiousity. Or were the fifteen volumes fifteen volumes of this smaller format?

Very shortly I'll be releasing my own book on self-publishing called *Getting Down and Digital: How to Self-publish Your Book*. It's primarily aimed at the book publishing audience, but many of the principles can be transferred to comics. Not so much self-publishing floppies, but graphic novels as I believe my publishing model is very sound and would even be of service to you should you wish to a) publish more *Collected Letters* volumes, b) the hinted-at-yet-never-committed-to volume of *Collected Essays*, b) any foray into fiction you might do down the road.

I'll be sure to send you a copy once I get my own stock here at the studio.

Thank you, by the way, for suggesting to have Tim Webber run "A 21st Century Guide To Self-Publishing In 8 Easy-To-Follow Steps" on *A Moment of Cerebus*. He did. I also co-ran it on my own website at www.canisterx.com

Unfortunately, I haven't followed my own system as I found some faults, namely due to the nature of the single-issue comic book market these days. I've devised some alternatives and plan on following that instead. Basically, it will be following the book model—which works as that's how I make my living—but instead of releasing the issues as twenty-pagers monthly, switch to a forty-pager (or so) bi-monthly, thus enabling to cost-effectively follow my book model and not lose money on every issue. Amazon.com would become my main storefront as opposed to the comic shops, though I'd solicit Diamond for when the graphic novel(s) come out. While I fully realize that it's common to lose money on a comic book for the first year or two, I just don't have that kind of money to spare. If I was single and had only me to worry about, I could probably swing it, but with a wife and kids, it's just not possible. The book model, however, slashes costs to next to nothing—literally—so that's more of a risk with the only potential loss being that of my time. This is another reason I want to send you the book because by having next-to-no-overhead other than your time, this might make things possible for you to put out other volumes of *Collected Letters* (even if just for me, harhar).

Enclosed with this letter is my half of the deal of our book trade. *The Axiom-man Saga* thus far in reading order: *Axiom-man*, *Episode No. 0: First Night Out*, *Doorway of Darkness*, *Episode No. 1: The Dead Land*, *City of Ruin*, *Axiom-man* Nos. 1-2. What is not included because they aren't printed in collected form (yet) are the three short stories so far written for the saga. Likewise, *Axiom-man* No. 3. While it's finished and most of it has aired on the Web, it's not here as I couldn't find a local printer to print up the comic for a decent cost at the quantity I needed (around three hundred copies). To have them printed out of town and then sent to me would destroy any chance of a profit per issue sold. I lost the first printer for the comic because, while they quoted me a good deal, they later said they lost money on the print run so didn't want to do it again. Lost the second printer because they botched up the job and had to rerun it so they didn't want to deal with me again. (It was their fault as their first trimming of issue two either trimmed off parts of the comic itself or didn't trim enough and left a white border around the book.) This is what prompted my looking into other options, the whole, "There has to be another way" and a something I've grown quite used to since beginning my publishing journey back in 2003 and my, what I call, "true" self-publishing journey in 2004. (In 2003 I subsidy/vanity published with another place; you know, the kind where you pay them a stupid amount of money only to sit on a bunch of books that won't sell. Ironically, it was this harrowing experience that made me fall in love with the publishing side of book making.)

As a one-man band, you need to simplify things and automate things so much so you can do things like, well, creating. Fortunately, my book model allows this. But then I got slowed down with other things like running the business as I also published other people for a time. I recently got out of that because it got to the point that more time was taken doing administration work than writing books.

Back when you started, you had Deni to help. Without meaning to step into forbidden territory, I'm curious how that worked?

Were you the creative guy and she ran the business side? What about when Aardvark-Vanaheim was publishing comics other than *Cerebus*? Did you have a hand in that or was that all Deni? I don't remember the timeline between when you split up and when Gerhard came aboard—was there a gap between the two? If so, how did you manage juggling making the book and the office side? I'm curious because if there are any tips you can give, I'm all ears as I'm always open to learning something. I'm finding that even after all this time doing this, my biggest problem is lack of schedule, that is, "Mon.-Thur. I'm creating, Friday is admin and marketing day." I tend to just "do what needs doing" but this isn't always the best plan of attack because something always needs doing.

Back to comics . . .

The comic market is changing like crazy thanks to so many people getting their comics digitally. It's one thing if you're DC or Marvel and have these proven properties with big names writing and drawing them, but a guy like me? Yeesh. Even with DC or Marvel, however, their sales on, say, *Superman,* are not near what they were a few years ago. I mean, they started The New 52 for a reason and, I suspect, being a marketing gimmick played a big part of it. I think I read somewhere that the idea was if The New 52 didn't take, it'd be a storyline they'd have in place for a year then return things to normal after. We're in year two now for The New 52, but if things start to peter out—I mean, DC's already canceled a bunch of books from the original line, started new ones, canceled those, started yet some more—then I suspect the whole "New 52 as a storyline" will be the play. I know guys like Mark Waid and Erik Larsen are constantly talking about new models and trying to figure out what works, what doesn't, and what to do. The competition is ridiculous because, for the most part, every Tom, Dick and Harry can publish their comic in some way (whether online, in print, etc). Unlike back when you started and the comic shops were it in terms of where to buy comics. (I think the direct market was around in 1977, right? I'm a little fuzzy on my comic history.)

Anyway, I guess I should explain what you're getting yourself into should you read *The Axiom-man Saga* and, really, if you don't, that's fine; they make excellent doorstops, bird cage liners, and fuel for bonfires. I'm honestly not seeking comment or endorsement or anything like that. Won't object, if you do, but that isn't my motivation in passing them along. Just making good on a trade as per your invite and also as a token of thanks for the inspiration to go my own way in terms of what I create.

The Axiom-man Saga is something of a childhood fantasy that I've had in my head since I was thirteenish. I used to deliver the paper for the *Winnipeg Free Press*. While going along my route, I'd launch myself into a whole superhero fantasy where I played the titular character. Made the time go by obscenely fast and oftentimes I had to go back and double check I delivered the paper to the houses on my list as I was so lost in my fantasy I wasn't sure if I did them or not. (Turns out I did put the papers in the mailbox out of sheer habit and repetition, but it goes to show the power of the imagination.) I did this for years (did papers on a couple of different routes from ages nine to eighteen). As a result, I have years of superhero stories in my head and have been putting them to paper in the form of *The Axiom-man Saga* as of 2006.

But in the end, what I'm trying to achieve with *The Axiom-man Saga* are several things, among which are a) something massive to leave to behind after I'm gone (I love epic stories), b) my personal "life's work," c) telling a superhero story on my own terms for good or ill, c) make a few bucks because I have to eat, too.

The *Axiom-man* storyline is set to be twenty-five full-length books, with twenty-five episodes in between each, making it fifty books total. Peppered throughout the series will be—and have been—short stories and comics. The full-lengthers are meant to be treated as feature films in terms of layers of storytelling and scope, the episodes being what the name implies—short "episodes," like a half-hour cartoon where you have one or two plotlines running and that's it. They all feed off each other, of course, as they're part of the greater whole, but each book has its own beginning, middle and end and a reader can easily pick up any one of them and have a good time. I came into this bizarre format/way of presenting the series by accident because in 2007 I wanted to do a short prequel to *Axiom-man*—which was an overlap tale that takes place between the "Four Months Ago . . ." sequences in *Axiom-man* and the main narrative—but it wasn't a long enough story to merit its own book, so it became "Episode 0" and that side of the overall Saga was born. If anything, the long-book-then-short-book format makes it unique, I suppose. This also gave birth to the cross-medium plan for the series, which further sets it apart.

It's a life-and-times superhero story, which goes against the grain of most superhero tales these days where it's little substance, lots of action, and forgettable storylines to deliver little substance and lots of action. It's also told from the point-of-view of, "If this happened tomorrow in our reality, how would it most realistically play out?" That was one of the things that made *Watchmen*, and more recently, *Kick Ass*, so successful: real superheroes in the real world. Granted, the heroes in those stories were didn't have superpowers (Dr. Manhatten aside) and thus "real" in that way, whereas Axiom-man has powers, but the main thrust is the same. I really play up the human side of my hero and try to have him handle things as realistically as possible given who he is as a person. Sometimes he handles them in a very spectacular way, others times not. Whatever best fits the situation.

Hollywood notions aside, I think that if a superpowered superhero showed up tomorrow—as there already are many non-superpowered superheroes at work in our world (not sure if you've heard of The Real Life Superhero Movement or not, but these guys are in costumes, are active and are making a difference)—I think that it wouldn't be as spectacular as most people think. I mean, a guy with powers wouldn't have much to do aside from stopping petty crimes if he happened upon them. If he was tenacious, he'd have a Batman side to him and would seek out stuff happening in the underground and infiltrate those operations. If a supervillain did show up, the villain would probably do this own thing until the superhero started interfering and only then would he seek to stop the good guy. And even then he probably wouldn't make a big work out of the superhero unless the superhero was constantly on his case about whatever evil things he was doing. Then it'd be all bets are off until the superhero is either incapacitated or dead.

So there you go, in a nutshell, what to expect from *The Axiomman Saga* should it become part of your reading schedule.

I was particularly intrigued by your cover to *Collected Letters Vol. 2*, namely that it was you, Chester Brown and Harvey Pekar. I'm a Harvey Pekar fan, having discovered him—as most people—through the *American Splendor* movie (which is an all-time favorite of mine and highly recommend watching it if you haven't already. Though I know TV isn't your thing, this flick is certainly worth the exception). I'm curious as to how you knew him or if that lunch was a one-off, or what the history is there? I remember seeing a strip about that same lunch—I think it was on *A Moment of Cerebus*—and you have a caption with an arrow pointing to Harvey saying, "So intense you can actually feel him reading" or something. Haha. Made me laugh as he really seems like that kind of guy (and we all have met at least one person who is intense like that even if just in presence). It's real sad that he passed on so soon, and by accident as well. By accident, I'm referring to the drug overdose but I also realize each of our days are numbered as per the Psalms and Harvey left right when he was supposed to. They recently made a memorial for him at the Cleveland Library in the form of a statue.

Harvey's comics are really good. A real celebration of the mundane, and while a lot of them see to just stop versus have actual endings, that's life for you, right? A lot of things . . . just. Stop.

Happened to Harvey.

Onto your letter from Christmas Eve, 2012:

You don't remember me, or, at least, the real version of me. Maybe the mention of *The Axiom-man Saga* triggered something, I don't know. I never lived in England. Winnipeg, Manitoba, born and raised and still living in. No big deal.

On the autobio thing ala Eddie Campbell: While I realize that sex, drugs and booze were the lifestyle of the old Dave and you don't want to bring up stories from those times, are there not other stories from that time period—pre-1996—that don't include those things? i.e. Stories from comic conventions during the '80s, or funny moments in the studio between you and Gerhard, or other life stuff? Even Dave-Sim-post-Bible stories are appealing—to me, anyway, as I'm an Evangelical Christian. I mean, life stuff, you know? I'm also a sucker for getting behind-the-scenes of cartoonists I admire and enjoy the works of Alec Longstreth (who sends you stuff), John Porcellino, Julia Wertz and others as a result.

Speaking of conventions, do you still do them? I thought I read somewhere recently that you did a show in New York or something? I thought The Last Signing was it or have you changed your mind? I ask because I'm friends with the owners of the Central Canada Comic Con that takes place in Winnipeg every fall and would have no trouble urging them to invite you down as a guest. Some 30,000 people attend that show. I table there every year.

Anyway, I'm running on four pages now and I still have a friend's book to edit this afternoon so I'm off. Hope you're keeping well and thanks again for sending *Collected Letters Vol. 2*. Very nice of you.

Take care, Dave.

Best,

Ps. Should you reply, feel free to save yourself a stamp and have Tim Webber email it to me at coscomentertainment@gmail.com, unless you do email these days then by all means feel free to contact me directly. Have a good one.

About the Author

A.P. Fuchs is the author of many novels and short stories. His most recent books are *Redemption of the Dead*, the third book in his zombie trilogy, *Undead World*; *Axiom-man: City of Ruin*; the paranormal romance series *Blood of my World*; and *Zombie Fight Night: Battles of the Dead*, in which zombies fight such classic monsters as werewolves, vampires, Bigfoot, and even go up against awesome foes like pirates, ninjas, and Bruce Lee. Also a cartoonist, he is known for his superhero series, *The Axiom-man Saga*, both in novel and comic book format.

Please see **www.axiom-man.com** for more on this series. Fuchs's main website is **www.canisterx.com**

www.ingramcontent.com/pod-product-compliance
Lightning Source LLC
Chambersburg PA
CBHW031232210726
48287CB00003B/758

* 9 7 8 1 9 2 7 3 3 9 4 3 5 *